Success Factors of Young African-American Males at a Historically Black College

Success Factors of Young African-American Males at a Historically Black College

Marilyn J. Ross

BERGIN & GARVEY
Westport, Connecticut • London

Library of Congress Cataloging-in-Publication Data

Ross, Marilyn J.
    Success factors of young African-American males at a historically
black college / Marilyn J. Ross.
        p.   cm.
    Includes bibliographical references (p.   ) and index.
    ISBN 0–89789–535–5 (alk. paper)
    1. Afro-American men—Education (Higher)   2. Afro-American college
students—Social conditions.   3. Afro-American universities and
colleges.   4. Academic achievement—United States.   I. Title.
LC2781.R66   1998   97–37560
378.1'982996'073—DC21

British Library Cataloguing in Publication Data is available.

Library of Congress Catalog Card Number: 97–37560
ISBN: 0–89789–535–5

First published in 1998

Bergin & Garvey, 88 Post Road West, Westport, CT 06881
An imprint of Greenwood Publishing Group, Inc.

Printed in the United States of America

The paper used in this book complies with the
Permanent Paper Standard issued by the National
Information Standards Organization (Z39.48–1984).

10 9 8 7 6 5 4 3 2

Copyright Acknowledgments

The author and publisher gratefully acknowledge permission to use the following materials.

"Mother to Son" from *Collected Poems* by Langston Hughes. Copyright © 1994 by the Estate of
Langston Hughes. Reprinted by permission of Alfred A. Knopf Inc. and Harold Ober Associates Inc.

Figures 2.1 and 3.1 from B. F. Crabtree and W. L. Miller (eds.), *Doing Qualitative Research.* Copyright © 1992 by Sage Publications, Inc. Reprinted by permission of Sage Publications, Inc.

To
Michael I. Ross
My husband and best friend
and
To our family
Sharyn Leslie and Jeffrey, Kathryn Anya and Alexander Forrest
Andrew Dean and Andee Hope, Miller Shea

Contents

Acknowledgments

I wish to express grateful appreciation to Dr. Albert E. Smith, president of Florida Memorial College, and to Dr. Karl S. Wright, vice president for Academic Affairs, for having the confidence and trust in me to represent the college in this undertaking.

A project in narrative inquiry can only be successful if the individuals involved in the study share their experiences, beliefs, and feelings. Because the men I interviewed in The President's Men program were serious about sharing their lives with me, this study became meaningful. I wish to thank each one of the thirty-four students who took part in this study and who, in my view, made a significant contribution to the literature regarding the experiences of black males.

I wish to give special acknowledgment to two Florida Memorial College colleagues whose encouragement and supportive assistance were indispensable to this project: Roscoe Warren, director of The President's Men program, who gave his consent for me to interview the men in his program and who gave me constant feedback throughout the study. His office door was always open to me, he had complete trust in me, and he was as enthusiastic about the project as I was. Professor Sandra T. Thompson was my mentor. From the beginning of the project, she patiently listened to my ideas and encouraged me. She would always interrupt her own busy schedule to answer my questions. Both of these colleagues were vital to a successful project. They gave validity to the study by corroborating that the emerging themes were an integral part of the black culture.

Faculty members whose advice I sought and who gave of their time and expertise were: Professors William E. Hopper, Charles C. Clency, Alvin L. Pondexter, Alfred Parker, Earl H. Duval, Albert H. McGhee, and Nina Gorman. Two counselors at the college assisted me: Vincent Ashley confirmed particular findings, and Dwight

Marshall became the coordinator for information that I requested on the sample group. I also wish to express my appreciation to Professor Donald G. Meagher, Miami-Dade Community College, for sharing his experiences and proficiency in qualitative research. I wish to commend the various libraries and staffs that expedited my research: the Florida Memorial College Library with special appreciation to Dr. Laban Connor, Sadie Smith, Sadie Reyes, and Leroy Thompson. I discovered that the Florida Memorial College Library, and its black archive section, has unsurpassed black studies material. Other libraries in which I spent many hours, days, and weeks were the University of Miami Library, the Florida International University Library, the Mid-Manhattan Library, and the Schomburg Center for Research and Black Culture in Harlem.

I wish to express my gratitude to Sanford J. Smoller, whose helpful suggestions and skill in editing made me feel at ease with the completed manuscript.

A special "thank you" goes to Desrene Stewart and Patrick Hylton, whose expertise on the computer polished the first draft of this book, and to Trevor Walker, who made my life easier when I needed assistance in duplicating material.

I wish to express my indebtedness to University of Miami professors who critiqued the early drafts of this study and who gave me insightful issues to explore. Because these various topics were reflected upon and researched, they gave the manuscript clarity and depth. Specifically, I want to thank Professor E. John Kleinert, whose gentle, kind manner and confidence in me gave me the courage to continue with the project. I wish to thank Professor John H. Croghan who set the groundwork for this book in his doctoral seminar on proposal writing and for always being in his office when I needed assistance. I also wish to thank Professor Hollis Price, who made me aware that statistical information could enhance a qualitative study, and Professor Robert F. Moore, who showed confidence in me and made helpful suggestions from the outset. I also owe special gratitude to Professor Kathleen A. Shea for insightful critiquing of the first draft and for her strong support of my efforts in scholarly pursuits.

I wish to acknowledge Jane Garry, acquisitions editor, Greenwood Publishing Group, for having confidence in the project. And most of all, I want to thank Michael I. Ross, whose interest in the study never wavered.

Success Factors of Young African-American Males at a Historically Black College

1

Introduction

THE NEED FOR ROLE MODELS FOR INNER-CITY BLACK YOUTHS

Researchers in the social sciences have well documented the critical need for successful black males to serve as role models for inner-city black youths. In the United Negro College Fund (UNCF) publication *Research Trends* (1988–89), for example, an article on black male college students noted that a "disproportionately high number of black males are raised in female-headed households with relatively few male role models present" (p. 3). Green (1991) confirmed that "one of the most crucial psychosocial deficits in the environment of inner city black male youth is the lack of consistent, positive and literate African-American male role models" (p. 12). As Gary Orfield, head of the Metropolitan Opportunity Project at the University of Chicago, observed in *Research Trends*, "One of the problems is that young black males really don't have any contact with successful black males who have been to college. They have more contact with those who have been successful in the underground economy" (p. 1).

Majors and Billson (1992) discussed the fact that although many black males are successful, not enough of these success stories are documented. Historically, investigators in the social sciences have emphasized negative aspects of black males, resulting in the examination of the African-American male from a deficit viewpoint. In order to bring success factors of the black male "close to home" for inner city youth, this study investigated and documented those special strengths and skills that a group of successful black male college students utilized to overcome economic and social hardships in pursuing their goals. As a result of the students' persistence, they are well on their way to assuming leadership roles in society. Through naturalistic inquiry, the study sought to answer what inner qualities compel some black males to persist and overcome adversity, while others of their socio-economic class quit and fail.

Little research has been done on successful black male college students. Majors and Billson (1992) found that "only a few studies explore the lives of successful African-American men who live complex, middle-class or professional lives with extended involvement in family, community, and national arenas" (p. 106). Not only have there been few studies of mature, successful black males, but there is also a paucity of research wherein young black males narrate their own life stories. Edwards and Polite (1992) supported the idea that in order for the young black person to achieve, it is critical "to focus on the success stories within the black race to identify the special strengths and skills it takes to prevail" (p. 4).

PURPOSE OF THE STUDY

One purpose of this study was to add to the limited research on successful black males; a second purpose was to determine that positive role models for black male adolescents do exist. The research was designed to identify the factors that led to the successful achievement of African-American male students at a 118-year-old, historically black college. Because too often individuals outside of the mainstream culture go unheard, the students in the study have narrated their own stories, including the obstacles that they had to overcome to reach success, as well as the support systems that assisted them along the way. In keeping with the twofold purpose, this study has documented the traits of seventeen African-American men who were members of an honorary organization called "The President's Men."

Although the study's primary thrust was to document the factors that led to African-American students' success, the sample group also included seventeen black male students who were born outside of the United States. Including these students in the interview process offered the opportunity to describe distinguishing characteristics of the two groups and to discover themes that were common to both. It also allowed for establishing themes that unite them.

LIMITS OF THE STUDY

Because this study employed naturalistic inquiry, the emerging data were not quantitatively tested or operationalized (except for demographics); this might be seen as a limitation. However, triangulation was used to substantiate the findings, as Lincoln and Guba (1985) emphasized. Sources used for triangulation are noted in the section on methodology.

Another limitation may be that not all of the male students who met the criteria for The President's Men were members of the program. Many students prefer not to join groups, and many students are involved in other activities; therefore, the sample is limited only to those students who were members, and it does not include all of the student population who may have met the criteria for membership. One should also keep in mind that African-American men do achieve even without a college degree. This study, therefore, should be seen as a microcosm of success stories within the black male population.

Additionally, readers should also be aware that the results of a qualitative study may not be highly generalizable or easily replicated. However, as this study was based on a specific set of questions, one can conjecture that it and its research methods could be replicated.

DEFINITION OF TERMS

Cluster I: Students born within the boundaries of the Continental United States.

Cluster II: Students born outside of the Continental United States.

Historically Black Colleges/Universities (HBCU): Colleges and universities that were established for the purpose of educating black youth at the postsecondary level.

SIGNIFICANCE OF THE STUDY

This study may be an inspiration for young African-American males, as well as those black male students born outside the United States, who feel that they have little or no chance for success. As there is a critical need for successful black males to serve as positive images for inner-city youth, this group of college students could provide role models for many disillusioned young African Americans. In a similar capacity, the college students could also serve as mentors to counsel and steer inner-city adolescents into setting goals in education.

2

Review of the Literature

This chapter includes narratives of African-American men who persisted in spite of the odds, literature depicting the black male as in crisis, the significance of role models and mentors, recent trends in higher education for African Americans, and the design of the study.

THE PERSEVERANCE OF THE BLACK MALE

Because narrative technique is fundamental to naturalistic inquiry, two illustrations were excerpted from *Ebony*. These vignettes were of African-American men who persevered in spite of the odds, and who could thereby serve as archetypes for disaffected young black men.

Thomas A. Fleming, the 1992 National Teacher of the Year Award winner, told his story in *Ebony* (1992). He was a former Detroit high school dropout, a "delinquent and illiterate youngster . . . abandoned by his mother, left to the care of his grandparents . . . frequently kicked out of school" (p. 70). While serving as a soldier overseas, he shared his illiteracy problem with a Bible study group on a base in France, and he eventually learned to read. After he returned home, education became the focus of his life. He earned his General Educational Development (GED) diploma, a bachelor's degree in religious education, and a master's degree in special education. He related that his childhood experiences helped him to reach out to his students, and that success for him was the students' awareness of their own worth.

In another article, by Booker (1988), "Black General at the Summit of U. S. Power," Colin Powell, former chairman of the Joint Chiefs of Staff—who grew up in the South Bronx, the son of a factory shipping foreman—defined success:

"Success is the result of perfection, hard work, learning from failure, loyalty to those for whom you work, and persistence" (p. 146). The black male students in this study could function as archetypes as well.

THE AFRICAN-AMERICAN MALE "IN CRISIS"

Although this study investigated the factors contributing to the African-American male students' success at a historically black college, it cites a sample of literature depicting the predicament of the black male to establish the groundwork of the problem: the facts of unemployment, unequal access into the American mainstream, and unprecedented numbers of black males in prison. These facts have been documented in scholarly studies that refer to the black male as the "vanishing black male" and as being "in crisis."

Prothrow-Stith (1993) remarked that young black males in prison outnumber those that are in college: "Approximately one in four African-American males between the ages of 20 and 29 is incarcerated, on probation, or on parole[;] . . . only one in five is enrolled in a two- or four-year college program" (p. 163). West (1994) reported on

the murky waters of despair and dread that now flood the streets of black America . . . the depressing figures of unemployment, infant mortality, incarceration, teenage pregnancy, and violent crime . . . the monumental eclipse of hope, the unprecedented collapse of meaning, the incredible disregard for human (especially black) life and property in much of black America . . . the profound sense of psychological depression, personal worthlessness, and social despair. (pp. 19–20)

A sense of alienation and isolation has long existed in the inner city. These themes have been written about by African-American novelists, such as Richard Wright in *Native Son* (1940) and Ralph Ellison in *The Invisible Man* (1952). Moreover, these themes of alienation and isolation were central in Andrew Hacker's groundbreaking study, *Two Nations: Black and White, Separate, Hostile, Unequal* (1992).

Hacker (1992) stated that in contrast to American society as a whole, the majority of young black men in America have been brought up in disadvantaged circumstances, perpetuating an inability to escape their surroundings or envision meaningful futures. In *Children of the Dream* (1992), Edwards and Polite noted that "success has always been a relative phenomenon in black America . . . often measured as much by what has been overcome as by what has been achieved" (p. 3).

Majors and Billson (1992) supported Edwards's and Polite's thesis that the African-American male has inordinate difficulties in his pursuit of success. The researchers addressed the problem of racism in American society, which, they argued, has blocked opportunities. Consequently, many of the images of a "successful black male" for black youth in the inner city are individuals who have chosen paths of nonconformity.

Another facet of black youths' predicament is single-parent homes. Ascher (1991), citing research on single-parent African-American homes, stated that the percentage of African-American families headed by a woman increased from 22 to 44 percent in the years between 1960 and 1985, and recorded information from a Morehouse College Community Service Project:

Half of these children have never visited their father's home. More than forty percent do not see their father at all in a typical year. Only one in five sleeps in a father's home in a typical month. In short, more and more of these children simply do not know what it means to have a father. (p. 4)

Ascher noted that "high unemployment forces these men into alternative economics. . . . While many are employed irregularly or not at all, others make money by selling drugs or being involved in risky and illegal work" (p. 5).

THE LACK OF MALE ROLE MODELS IN THE INNER CITY

In an article entitled "Black Youth, Role Models and the Social Construction of Identity," Taylor (1989) cited Keniston (1968; 1971), Erikson (1959), and others who assert that "choice and commitment" are major themes during the adolescent's struggle for identity formation (p. 157). As the adolescent prepares himself for an adult role in society, he "shops" around for the individual he wishes to emulate. The adolescent at this stage is "in search of identity," and "he seeks someone to follow" (p. 158).

However, Taylor's study found that many black male youths in the inner city do not have confidence and trust in others in their social environment. Taylor referred to Erickson (1968), who asserted that the lack of confidence and trust results from the adolescent's feelings of being deprived, of having been forsaken by significant others, as well as by society at large. Taylor also cited Kenneth Clark (1965), who commented more than twenty years ago that someone needs to care enough to give a sustained effort to black youth in the inner city, if they are to have an opportunity for a better future.

THE SIGNIFICANCE OF ROLE MODELS

Steel (1991), in "Mentoring: An Effective Tool for Retention of Minorities," presented an example of the way in which positive role models affect black youth. The researcher used an analogy to Thoreau's lines, "People will be what they see," and observed that there is currently a positive relationship between the numbers of black faculty at predominantly white institutions and recruitment, admissions, and graduation rates of black students. The research also showed that it was crucial for the student's success that the black faculty be available to serve as role models.

THE SIGNIFICANCE OF MENTORSHIP

The word *mentor* has its roots in classical Greek literature; it means "steadfast and enduring." An illustration of the meaning of mentor can be seen in Homer's *Odyssey*, wherein the Greek poet gave the name Mentor to a character who guides and educates Odysseus' young son (Mahoney, 1993). Mahoney narrated another example of a successful mentoring relationship:

> When Babe Ruth was a seven-year-old in Baltimore, his parents, who ran a waterfront saloon and had little time for their son, placed him in St. Mary's Industrial School. Much later, Babe Ruth wrote, "It was at St. Mary's that I met and learned to love the greatest man I have ever known. His name was Brother Matthias." Baseball's gain—and society's—was that Brother Matthias' special interest in Ruth gave him the encouragement he needed to play baseball and eventually to leave St. Mary's to play professionally. (p. 3)

Mahoney advised that "without support, young men . . . with the potential to climb up and out—fall back into a street culture that promises only hopelessness" (p. 5).

Weber (1992), in an interview with Jacqueline Fleming, recorded her response to the importance of mentoring for minority students: "When students can plug into someone who encourages them, this interaction can be an important part of the college experience and a source of inspiration. . . . Mentoring has also been associated with higher grade point averages" (p. 24).

A *New York Times* article, of December 1, 1996, reported on the present success represented by the University of Virginia's graduation rate (84 percent) for black students. The university has a support system in place, including "peer advisers, faculty mentors, a parents' advisory association, . . . [and] personal touches like a birthday card for every freshman from a dean's office."

Elam (1989) cited several other predominantly white universities that established successful mentoring programs to enhance comfort level and student learning for minorities in order to increase retention. Upon entrance to the university, students were assigned to professors or older students who were designated mentors. These institutions were the Cleveland State University, which developed a Minority Mentoring Program, and Ohio University, Athens, which instituted a Faculty Mentoring Program. Research at Ohio University and other institutions demonstrated that the student's relationship to the faculty would determine his or her level of belonging. The black student has to feel accepted, supported, and encouraged, especially in predominantly white institutions.

Florida Memorial College, the site of this study, has a mentoring program called "Shepherd's Watch." Its initial thrust came from the president of the college, Dr. Albert E. Smith; a task force was assembled that included all the chairpersons of the divisions. Training modules were developed, and more than seventy faculty and staff members were trained in the fundamentals of mentoring. In the spring of 1996, each mentor was assigned three protégés. The mentors were encouraged to meet with their protégés each week—to have lunch together, to attend college activities, and to get to know one another. Shepherd's Watch falls under the umbrella of

Student Support Services; in an interview, Shelton H. Allwood, director of Student Support Services and coordinator of the Shepherd's Watch Program, emphasized the role of senior students, who also serve as mentors to the freshmen and sophomore students. In this way, the model for "students helping students" is set in motion, and the senior student also benefits, by gaining the positive feeling of "giving back." In this sense, the Shepherd's Watch Program has two dimensions: faculty/staff and protégés, and "students helping students."

Although Shepherd's Watch is in its infant stage, student feedback has been positive, and future plans for the program include a reception at the beginning of the school year where mentors and protégés can meet, sponsored picnics, bowling trips, and other recreational activities to solidify the bond between mentor and protégé.

BLACK COLLEGES VERSUS WHITE COLLEGES FOR THE BLACK STUDENT

In a study entitled "Comparative and Predictive Analysis of Black and White College Achievement and Experiences," Nettles, Thoeny, and Gosman (1986) recorded a relevant finding that student/environment fit is essential for academic success. This "person x environment fit" has positive results on students' achievement. Students need to feel comfortable in their environment, both academically and socially; they need to perceive the college as nondiscriminatory; and they need to feel academically integrated.

The research indicated that certain factors have a negative bearing upon black students' college performance, such as their greater likelihood to have attended public high schools (while white students have a proclivity to attend private high schools); their greater tendency to live off campus (while white students tend to live on campus); and their greater likelihood of attending a university where they are in the racial minority.

In another study, "African-American College Student Outcomes at Predominantly White and Historically Black Public Colleges and Universities" (Allen, 1992), the findings indicated that black students who attend black colleges have benefits beyond what the white institutions can provide to black students. These benefits are manifested in "positive psychological adjustments, more significant academic gains, and greater cultural awareness/commitment than black students on white campuses. . . . The 'fit' between African-American students and higher education seems more favorable on historically Black campuses than on predominantly White campuses" (p. 32). Allen also observed, however, that the parents of black students who attend historically black institutions have less formal education, fewer prestigious jobs, and less economic means than both black and white students who attend predominantly white institutions.

Allen (1992) noted that relevant differences in outcome exist for African-American students who attend a historically black college (HBCU) vis-à-vis African-American students who attend a predominantly white institution (PWI). The social-psychological context must be taken into account in order for black students to be successful in higher education. On white campuses, "black students emphasize feelings of alienation, sensed hostility, racial discrimination, and lack of integration, [but] . . . on historically Black campuses, Black students emphasize feelings of engagement, connection, acceptance, and extensive support and encouragement" (p. 39).

Allen concluded his research by summarizing the results of previous studies for factors associated with black student success in college. The important factors are financial support, adequate academic preparation, and academic remediation, if necessary. Significant additional factors are improving college academic support services and redressing the negative impact of hostile racial and social relationships—for "when black students are made to feel unwelcome, incompetent, ostracized, demeaned, and assaulted, their academic confidence and performance understandably suffer" (p. 41).

Steward, Jackson, and Jackson (1990) asserted that when black students on white campuses reach out to white students, it is mainly for an interchange of information relating to academic and professional success; therefore, the interaction between black and white students is less socially motivated than goal oriented. Successful black students in a PWI are "loners"; because they want to obtain their degree and get on with life, their purpose at the PWI is to further their professional ambitions and obtain access to the mainstream. These students have the capacity to survive without the emotional attachments that are usually made in a college environment; the black students who need emotional attachment do not survive the four years at the PWI. Steward, Jackson, and Jackson referred to Beckham's (1988) study, which concluded that the environment for black students is such at PWI that they feel like "strangers in a strange land" (p. 515). The results of the Steward study suggest that even those students who fit academically remain "alien" interpersonally. Black students at PWI adapt to remaining a "stranger" and retreat from emotional situations that might contribute to their academic demise.

Schoem (1991) argued that an in-depth, thoughtful study of race relations needs to be incorporated into the college curriculum. In his own classes at the University of Michigan he observed that students are anxious to discuss and study intergroup conflict and social change. In classes on intergroup relations students become open and honest, facing their own prejudices and seeing, perhaps for the first time, the other group's perspective.

McEwen, Roper, Bryant, and Langa (1990) identified nine factors that relate to developmental tasks of the black student: developing racial identity, interacting with the mainstream culture, developing cultural awareness, developing self-identity, developing interdependence, fulfilling affiliation needs, surviving intellectually, surviving spiritually, and developing social responsibility.

These specific psychological and social needs create conflicts for the young black student trying to cope within the PWI (as well as to make the grade academically). For example, black students may have insecurities because of their ethnic identity and therefore have to put a great deal of psychological energy into protecting themselves against emotional upheaval in order to survive the semester intact. Another obstacle for black students is the complex task of adjusting to a campus environment different from their own cultural frame of reference.

Fleming (1991) referred to Gurin and Epps (1975), who "maintain that many black students will still prefer to attend [black] colleges where the campus ambience supports their personal development without the level of conflict and isolation experienced on many predominantly white campuses" (p. 9). Fleming asserted that the profile of black males attending white institutions can be characterized as *grim*. The black male experiences frustrating incidents that impede his academic drive; the result is "falling grades, diminishing feelings of intellectual ability, declining social adjustment, and losses in perceived energy level . . . [which are] symbolic of their psychological withdrawal" (p. 169).

In contrast to the grim picture described above, Fleming's research on the impact of college on black students showed that

males in black schools exhibit the happiest adjustment to college life that can be found. Despite some ambivalence surrounding their interactions with teachers, their experience is more strongly characterized by absorption with role models, greater satisfaction with and positive outcomes from the educational experience (including perceived cognitive growth), and gains in assertiveness of self-expression and in dealing with others. (p. 168)

Weber asked Fleming to comment on her research regarding African-Americans in historically black institutions and predominantly white institutions. Fleming replied,

Now we see that the interpersonal environment has more to do with achievement and development. Students in HBIs have access to a wider network of relationships that are friendly, that make them feel as if they belong, and that encourage and inspire them onto greater heights. It is the "people factor" in education that I think has long been ignored and turns out to distinguish the experience of African-American students in historically black institutions from that in predominantly white institutions. (p. 21)

The black college experience for the black student is a positive one, in that it is a nurturing environment; faculty members at black colleges discern students' difficulties and take the time to help them progress.

TRENDS IN HIGHER EDUCATION FOR AFRICAN AMERICANS

Feagin, Vera, and Imani (1996) examined black and white college enrollment figures from the late 1960s to the 1990s and reported that the percentage of black high school graduates attending college increased from the late 1960s to the late 1970s. The percentages of black and white students enrolled in college were not noticeably different during the early 1970s, when 27 percent of black high school graduates were enrolled in college, compared with 30 percent of white high school graduates. Nonetheless, gradual changes in college enrollment were taking place. In the ten-year span from the 1980s to the 1990s, the gap between white enrollment figures and black enrollment figures widened. In 1993, for example, nearly 41 percent of whites and 33 percent of blacks were enrolled in college, but the retention rate for African-American students was significantly lower than that for white students. The study cited Arnold Mitchem, executive director of the National Council of Educational Opportunity Associations, as reporting that the graduation rate for African Americans after six years was 32 percent and for whites after six years 56 percent.

Not only was the retention rate dropping, but college enrollment for blacks was plummeting. Carnoy (Winter 1994/1995) explained that a principal reason for the drop in college enrollment of blacks was that government policy toward funding higher education had dramatically changed. College financial grants were reduced from 80 percent in 1975–76 to 50 percent in 1985–86. The new government policy, which decreased grants and established a system of loans, affected black enrollment, particularly because the change occurred at a time when tuition costs at state colleges and universities increased.

Feagin, Vera, and Imani (1996) cited not only the above reason for the drop in enrollment of black students in higher education but also other factors, such as offers of good positions in the military for blacks, and the general uneasiness felt by black students about pursuing an education in white colleges and universities. Interviewing minority students at PWIs, Feagin, Vera, and Imani found that black students perceived no significant support structure in place that would give them a sense of belonging in a culture that was predominantly white. They discovered just the opposite—that predominantly white universities do not make any effort to address the needs of the black student. One black student commented that whites "just want us sitting there" to prove that the university is adhering to the affirmative action program.

However, contrary to the above, when blacks entered prestigious colleges and universities, statistics in *The Journal of Blacks in Higher Education* (Autumn 1996) revealed, the 1995 graduation rates for black students approached or exceeded 90 percent in universities such as Harvard (95 percent), Yale (89 percent), and Princeton (91 percent). The select black students enrolled are successfully competing with white students.

The same issue of *The Journal of Blacks in Higher Education* also identified colleges and universities that have black graduation rates of 70 percent or higher. Representative examples were Holy Cross (87 percent), Colgate (82 percent), Bucknell (79 percent), and Duquesne (71 percent). The journal also listed the graduation rates of black students at southern state universities. These state-supported institutions enroll thousands of black students each year. Although their graduation rates are lower than those of the universities named above, the percentages of black and white students that graduate from these universities located in the South are noteworthy: the University of Virginia was ranked first, with a graduation rate for blacks of 84 percent and for whites 93 percent. Other southern schools listed were the University of South Carolina, with a graduation rate for blacks of 56 percent and for whites 63 percent; the University of Georgia, with a graduation rate for blacks of 52 percent and for whites 62 percent; and the University of Mississippi, with a graduation rate for blacks of 46 percent and for whites 49 percent. In order to be included in these statistics, students had to have entered the university from 1986 to 1989 and have graduated within six years of their original enrollment. (The article also stated that the students enrolled in these universities are academically equivalent in their qualifications.)

The above statistics do not have a breakdown of male/female findings. The picture becomes clearer from reports such as Slater (1994). His research found that African-American women enrolled in college are the reason for the gains in black enrollment figures. Black women eclipse black men in practically all statistical measurements in postsecondary education. Slater stated that thirty years ago, black men who finished high school were far more likely to go on to college than were black women. Currently, black men are falling behind black women in almost every assessment of progress in higher education.

Nettles's (1997) investigation of African-American data for the Frederick D. Patterson Research Institute of the College Fund/UNCF reported that between 1976 and 1994 more black women than black men entered colleges and universities nationally. In the fall of 1994, for example, 898,605 African-American women versus 549,603 African-American men enrolled in institutions of higher education—a disparity of 24 percent. Nettles's findings also revealed that although the number of bachelor's degrees granted to African-American men increased by 19.6 percent, from 25,147 in 1977 to 30,086 in 1994, the number granted to African-American women increased by 55.4 percent, from 33,489 in 1977 to 52,047 in 1994.

During this same interval, the number of bachelor's degrees awarded by HBCUs overall increased by 16.23 percent, from 23,551 in 1977 to 27,391 in 1994. The research and collected data show that HBCUs are an important factor in educating African Americans. In 1993 and 1994, for example, African Americans earned only 7 percent of bachelor's degrees at institutions of higher education nationwide; significantly, they earned 85.6 percent of bachelor's degrees at HBCUs (Nettles).

Nettles also noted that the number of African-American women who received master's degrees at institutions of higher education, including HBCUs, was about double the number of African-American men: 13,890 versus 7,002 at all institutions in 1994, and 2,248 versus 939 at HBCUs in 1994. With the same data, he addressed the number of doctoral degrees awarded between 1977 and 1994, which increased by 30 percent among all students—from 33,232 in 1977 to 43,185 in 1994. At HBCUs the number of doctoral degrees awarded between 1977 and 1994 increased by 218 percent among all students (from 66 in 1977 to 210 in 1994). For both whites and African Americans, the number of doctoral degrees earned by men decreased between 1977 and 1994, while the number awarded to women increased. The number of doctoral degrees awarded to African-American men declined by 20.5 percent, from 766 in 1977 to 609 in 1994, while the number awarded to African-American women increased by 50.9 percent, from 487 in 1977 to 735 in 1994. In

1994, African-American men constituted 1.4 percent of all doctorates awarded (down from 2.3 percent in 1977), while African-American women represented 1.7 percent (up from 1.5 percent in 1977).

If black men do not keep up with the achievements of black women in education, a growing gap between the African-American male and the female will eventually erode the relative earning power of the male and will undermine the black male's status in the family, and, in all probability, accelerate the breakdown of traditional black family life.

At the present time, 300,000 more black women attend college than black men. Since 1980 the disparity has grown by 78 percent. By 1991, 41,012 bachelor's degrees had been earned by black women, representing 62.8 percent of the total number of degrees earned by both black males and black females. If this trend continues, in a few years black women will earn two out of every three degrees.

The statistics indicate that black men are losing ground to black women in education. Slater (1994) emphasized that in recent years that trend seemed to be growing. From 1990 to 1992, the percentage of black men ages eighteen to twenty-four enrolled in college declined from 26.1 percent to 21.2 percent. Slater also reviewed the possible reasons why African-American men are faring so poorly in postsecondary education. He expressed the view that the black male felt that since he would probably not be hired because of his race, why should he spend the time preparing himself educationally for work? Slater also blamed the lack of a reliable male in the home to mentor the child; further, there are no black male role models in many elementary and secondary schools, and the black adolescent student sees a black person doing only menial tasks—such as janitorial—in many of the schools. Indeed, the only successful black men the young black male knows about are athletes, entertainers, or musicians—careers that do not require much formal education. According to Slater, school is seen by black youth as an authoritarian agency not worthy of respect, and many black adolescents feel hostility to education and have an anti-achievement ethic. Students who even attempt to be educationally motivated are isolated by their peers.

Garibaldi (1992) stated that the school system is apathetic to the African-American male. His article, "Educating and Motivating African-American Males to Succeed," documented research supporting his findings that contrary to public perception, the African-American male desires to finish school. In a study of 2,250 African-American males in a New Orleans school district, 95 percent reported that they expected to graduate from high school; 40 percent, however, responded that they believed that their teachers were indifferent to their achieving, and 60 percent of the African-American males in the study felt that their teachers should have higher expectations of them. Of a sample of 500 teachers (318 responded), asked if they had confidence that their black male students would pursue a college education, six out of ten replied negatively. Sixty percent of the teachers surveyed were elementary school teachers, 70 percent of them had ten or more years of experience, and 65 percent of them were black. Garibaldi wrote that teachers are

organizations persisted, not only through the leadership of black ministers but through the unwavering belief among blacks that in essence their progress had to remain in the hands of black leaders, and that the key to freedom and advancement was education.

In locations other than the South, black private colleges were founded before the Civil War. In 1854, Lincoln University in Pennsylvania was established by the Presbyterian church, and in 1856 Wilberforce University in Ohio was established by the Methodist Episcopal church. These two colleges remain in their original locations and are degree-granting institutions.

In 1861, the American Missionary Association (AMA) became a strong advocate for educating freed slaves. It established seven black colleges and thirteen normal schools between the years 1861 and 1870. The Freedman's Bureau, in operation until 1870, also guided freed blacks in preparation for their new roles in society (Willie and Edmonds, 1978).

An example of the philosophy of separate education for blacks was the founding in 1868 of Hampton Institute, the first historically black college, by General S. C. Armstrong. Even though northern missionaries espoused the view that blacks should have a liberal arts education, Armstrong was convinced that blacks were less competent than whites and that a vocational education was sufficient. This thinking—that blacks were inferior—corresponded with that of southern whites. Booker T. Washington, a student at Hampton Normal and Agricultural Institute (as it was then called), was later to adopt the same educational philosophy as Armstong. In 1895, Washington advocated practical training and vocational education in his "Atlanta Compromise" speech at the Atlanta Cotton Exposition. Although Washington may have taken this stance because he felt that there was a need for "accommodation" with southern whites, the result was government support of separate education for the races. In 1896, the Supreme Court upheld the doctrine of "separate but equal" in the case of *Plessy v. Ferguson.* The Plessy decision resulted in an increase in Jim Crow mandates, and violence against blacks escalated. President Woodrow Wilson carried separation of the races a step further by supporting segregation in government offices (Thomas, 1981).

The inauguration of Rutherford B. Hayes as president of the United States ended the Reconstruction Period (1867-1877). The government system of education was more egalitarian between the years 1863 to 1877, but when Republican legislators in the South were voted out of office after 1877, the quality of education for blacks spiraled downward. On the other hand, education for southern whites improved. The legislatures had additional tax revenue from black citizens, and they voted to put the extra funds into white education. Any egalitarian treatment for blacks in education was reversed, and the caste system was reinstated (Roebuck and Murty).

Feagin, Vera, and Imani (1996) noted that even when slavery ceased, legal segregation of African Americans in southern schools became the dominant system and that thirteen states outside the South, among them New York, Illinois, Indiana, and Ohio, legislated or permitted segregation. Public universities for blacks were established in several southern and border states following the second Morrill Act of August 30, 1890. The Morrill Act underscored industrial, mechanical, and agricultural training, setting in motion the legal separation of public colleges into black and white schools. Ultimately, all the schools established under the Morrill Act offered degrees, but it was the black private colleges that offered degrees in the liberal arts (Roebuck and Murty). By 1900, approximately thirty-five public and private black colleges had been established (Willie and Edmonds, 1978).

Public higher education in the United States did not reflect a democratic tradition, one that would allow students of all ethnic groups to enter the system without prejudice. By 1900 all southern states had legally segregated schools, and the majority of northern schools maintained a segregated policy built into school practice and local mores, continuing a system of institutionalized racism in education. Although the first black American graduated from Bowdoin College in 1826, it took more than sixty years, until 1890, to graduate thirty more black Americans from a white college or university (Feagin, Vera, and Imani).

Roebuck and Murty reported that during the years 1865 to 1890, the more than two hundred black private institutions established in the southern region of the United States included in their titles "normal," "college," or "university"; that largely elementary and secondary schools, they were financed mainly by the AMA, the Freedman's Bureau, and the black church. Historically black Florida Memorial College, the subject of the present study, was founded in 1879, and as can be seen in the following description, fits within this timeframe. Colleges referred to as "historically black colleges" were founded for the education of blacks before the 1954 Supreme Court ruling in *Brown v. Board of Education*.

When Booker T. Washington died in 1915, his philosophy of education for blacks waned. Blacks felt the necessity for an expanded curriculum in a society that was now less agricultural and more industrial, especially in the urban centers where many blacks had migrated. Elementary and secondary education in the historically black colleges were eliminated by 1928, and a college-level curriculum took their place. W.E.B. DuBois was an example of an educated black man who received his undergraduate degree at a black college and obtained his doctorate at a white university (Harvard). From 1895 to 1930, the illiteracy rate among blacks dropped from 60 to 25 percent. By 1939, 119 doctorates had been earned by blacks in white colleges and universities (Thomas, 1981).

Significant court rulings and government intervention on behalf of civil rights in the Desegregation Period (1954 to 1975) were the impetus for the outward inclusion of blacks within the system. The 1954 Supreme Court decision *Brown v. Board of Education* ruled that racial segregation in public schools deprived black students of equal protection under the Fourteenth Amendment of the Constitution. The decision reversed the "separate but equal" decision of 1896 *Plessy v. Ferguson* (Willie and Edmonds, 1978). Segregation was rendered unconstitutional by the Civil Rights Act of 1964, which prohibited the spending of federal funds for segregated schools and colleges. This mandate dismantled de jure segregation, but even the United States Supreme Court could not put an end to segregation in an orderly manner. Violence stemming from southern resistance became a part of

American life from 1955 to 1965. In 1969, the Supreme Court ruled in *Alexander v. Holmes County Board of Education* that school segregation had to cease at once. For fifty years, from 1930 until 1980, the South battled in and out of the courts to keep the segregated system intact (Roebuck and Murty, 1993).

Although many more African-American students are now enrolling in formerly all-white colleges and universities, HBCUs should remain an integral part of American higher education and retain their historically black identity. The steadfast roots of black culture, the poignancy of black history with its legacy of a suffering people, and the ardor of the black church—all are within the hallowed halls of the historically black college.

DESIGN OF THE STUDY

Initial Procedures

This study used a post-positivist approach to research called naturalistic inquiry. Naturalistic inquiry can be seen as a clean slate for investigating human subjects; there are no a priori assumptions. It acknowledges the relevance of primary sources; that is, individuals relate incidents from their own perspectives. Because of the holistic approach of naturalistic inquiry, the "human instrument," or researcher, is sensitive to the essence, or gestalt, of the situation. This type of research is ideographic, inductive, flexible, multilayered, holistic, context oriented, and theory-generating.

In naturalistic inquiry, the researcher "begins as an anthropologist might begin learning about a strange culture, by immersing himself in the investigation with as open a mind as possible, and permitting impressions to emerge" (Guba, 1978, p. 13).

Naturalistic inquiry has many designations, such as post-positivistic, ethnographic, phenomenological, subjective, case-study, qualitative, hermeneutic, humanistic, grounded theory, and constructed reality. The following factors within the boundaries of naturalistic inquiry are germane to this study.

Ethnography

In ethnographic research, according to Crabtree and Miller (1992), the researcher is an integral part of the ethnographic process and is "immersed in the everyday life of the culture being studied" in order to "identify the meanings, patterns, and passions of a bounded cultural group" (p. 27). Crabtree and Miller emphasized the importance of interpretation and stated that clarification of the emerging data must filter through two "worlds": the researcher's "worlds" of objectivity and subjectivity.

Phenomenology

Ethnography and phenomenology are interrelated concepts, in that the technique of phenomenology also seeks to comprehend the "experiences of individuals and their intentions within their 'lifeworld.' " (Crabtree and Miller, p. 14). The researcher must put aside biases and prejudices and immerse him- or herself in the respondents' sphere and "use the self as an experiencing interpreter." In other words, the researcher must endeavor to "stand in the shoes" of the respondent and seek to answer the question, "What is it like to have a certain experience?" (p. 24). The researcher must keep in mind that all data must be seen through the eyes of the respondent.

Hermeneutics

Crabtree and Miller (1992) included a chapter on "Grounded Hermeneutic Research," written by Richard B. Addison. Addison discussed hermeneutics, a technique beyond phenomenology. The word "hermeneutics" means "to enlighten" or "to interpret"; its main concern is the matter of clarification. The word alludes to the messenger god, Hermes, in classical Greek literature, who had the ability to translate the gods' messages to the mortals on earth. The practice of hermeneutics has a long tradition; the approach is used in analyzing written texts, such as "biblical exegesis, legal interpretation, and linguistic and literary analysis" (p. 110). Hermeneutic analysis is the means of translating a circumstance from "unintelligibility to understanding" (p. 110). The interviews in this study were analyzed according to themes. The analysis, therefore, can be envisioned as analogous to literary analysis.

Addison further stated that the "participants of research are meaning-giving beings . . . [and] meaning is not only that which is verbalized; meaning is expressed in action and practices. . . . He emphasized that the researcher should "look at everyday practices, not just beliefs about those practices" (p. 111). In other words, for proper analysis, the naturalistic inquirer should also examine "background conditions such as immediate context, social structures, personal histories, shared practices, and language" (p. 112). In this respect, through metaphoric analysis, the students' underlying actions and thoughts become apparent.

Addison listed practices that are the essence of this study:

1. Immersing oneself in the participants' world;
2. Looking beyond individual actions to a larger background context and its relationship to the individual events;
3. Entering into an active dialogue with the research participants;
4. Analyzing in a circular progression between parts and whole, foreground and background. (p. 113)

The techniques of phenomenology and hermeneutics work well together to meet the criteria of a holistic approach to naturalistic inquiry. Chapter 4, "Emergent Findings and Postreview of the Literature," integrates relevant historical and cultural information that provides a backdrop for understanding the human actions and phenomena discovered. Nevertheless, it is apparent that a blurring of boundaries exists within the branches of qualitative research.

Grounded Theory

"Grounded theory" refers to theory that is grounded in the data. Therefore, in qualitative research, the data must be collected first in order to establish inductively a hypothesis (a posteriori), contrary to the conventional method, which establishes the hypothesis first (a priori), then deductively endeavors to prove it. As Glaser and Strauss (1967) stated:

theory must fit the situation being researched, and work when put into use. By "fit" we mean that the categories must be readily (not forcibly) applicable to and indicated by the data under study[;] by "work" we mean that they must be meaningfully relevant to and be able to explain the behavior under study. (p. 3)

Chapter 4 demonstrates that the recorded themes are grounded in the direct responses of the students. Further interpretations were determined by the "constant comparative method."

Constant Comparative Method

In this type of research, an important part of data analysis is the "constant comparative method," whereby the researcher continually compares interpretations "in the form of 'memos' against the data" (Lincoln and Guba, 1985, p. 27). These "memos" are a type of "analytical notekeeping." Lincoln and Guba (1985) stressed that it is crucial for the researcher to draw comparisons; they quoted salient passages from the earlier insights of from Glaser and Strauss (1967).

This constant comparison of the incidents very soon starts to generate theoretical properties of the category. The analyst starts thinking in terms of the full range of types or continua of the category, its dimensions, the conditions under which it is pronounced or minimized, its major consequences, its relation to other categories, and its other properties. (p. 106)

Glaser and Strauss further explained that the evaluator will detect two groupings: those constructed by him- or herself and those emanating from the respondents:

As his theory develops, the analyst will notice that the concepts abstracted from the substantive situation will tend to be current labels in use for the actual processes and behaviors that are to be explained, while the concepts constructed by the analyst will tend to be the explanations. (Lincoln and Guba, 1985, p. 341)

Negative Case Analysis

In naturalistic inquiry, negative case analysis is useful for refining the hypotheses. The researcher must take into account "all known cases without exception" (Lincoln and Guba, 1985, p. 309). Sometimes, one must revise the hypotheses many times before coming to this stage of analysis: "A single negative case is enough to require the investigator to revise a hypotheses" (Lincoln and Guba, p. 310). In this study, a continued process of analysis occurred until the concept of "nurturing" emerged. This concept included all of the cases, and it emerged only after the themes were integrated and documented. This experience can be described as the "Ah ha!"—the breakthrough experience, an illumination of the critical question "What's happening here?" Therefore, as Lincoln and Guba observed, inductive analysis of the data is a constant "process of revising hypotheses with hindsight" (p. 309).

Constructed Realities

Naturalistic inquiry has often been referred to as "constructivist inquiry" (Crabtree and Miller, 1992, p. 10). Often, the term "constructivism" is used for this paradigm, because the researcher in fact interprets, assembles, and creates the reality from the data.

Lincoln and Guba (1985), in a chapter entitled "Constructed Realities," used an old Chinese proverb to illustrate the ongoing struggle with the philosophical concept of reality: "I fell asleep, and while sleeping, I dreamed that I was a butterfly. But when I awoke, I was uncertain whether I was a man dreaming that I was a butterfly, or whether I was a butterfly dreaming that I was a man, dreaming that I was a butterfly" (p. 70). They contended that reality is "chameleonlike" and that this changing quality of reality pervades all realms of consciousness. To further illustrate their point, they recalled a story about Jocko Conlan, a National League umpire, who had his own definition of baseball reality: "They ain't nothin' til I calls 'em" (p. 70).

Lincoln and Guba (1985) postulated that there are "an infinite number of constructions that might be made and hence there are multiple realities. . . . Each is undoubtedly incomplete or erroneous to some degree" (p. 84). However,

under this ontological position, the constructed realities ought to match the tangible entities as closely as possible, not, however, in order to create a derivative or reconstructed single reality (or fulfill the criterion of objectivity), but rather to represent the multiple constructions of individuals (or fulfill the criterion of fairness) . . . in general, group agreement determines truth. (p. 85)

Shiva's Circle

Crabtree and Miller (1992) also discussed "construct realities," and used a metaphor, "Shiva's Circle," to explain how a constructivist inquirer (or naturalistic inquirer) enters an interpretive circle. (See Figure 2.1.) Crabtree and Miller explained the metaphor of "Shiva's Circle":

Shiva is the androgynous Hindu Lord of the Dance and of Death. A constructivist inquirer enters an interpretive circle and must be faithful to the performance or subject, must be both apart from and part of the dance, and must always be rooted to the context. No ultimate truth

Figure 2.1
Shiva's Circle of Constructivist Inquiry

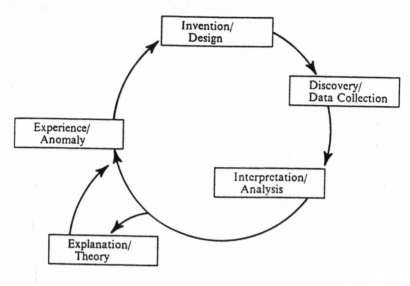

Source: From *Doing Qualitative Research* by B. F. Crabtree and W. L. Miller (eds.), 1992, Newbury Park, CA: Sage.

exists. . . . The constructivist inquirer enters into Shiva's Circle, performing an ongoing iterative dance of discovery and interpretation. (pp. 10, 11)

They explicated the process of "spiraling around the hermeneutic circle"—that there is a "circular movement of hermeneutic research from understanding to interpretation to deeper understanding to more comprehensive interpretation" (p. 118). It would be similar to "peeling an onion," layer by layer.

Trusting One's Own Knowledge

Glaser and Strauss (1965) in an article, "The Purpose and Credibility of Qualitative Research," included a section on trusting one's own credible knowledge. They discussed "why the fieldworker trusts what he knows" (p. 58):

The fieldworker knows what he knows, not only because he's been there in the field and because of his careful verification of hypotheses, but because "in his bones" he feels the worth of his final analysis. He has been living with partial analyses for many months, testing them each step of the way, until he has built his final analysis. What is more, if he has participated in the social life of his subjects then he has been living by his analyses, testing them out not only by observation and interview but also in daily livable fact. Hence by the close of his investigation, his conviction about his theory would be hard to shake. (p. 58)

In the present study, the following factors of qualitative research were utilized: ethnography, narrative inquiry, phenomenology, hermeneutics, grounded theory, constant comparative method, analytic memos, and constructivism. These components led to a comprehensive analysis of the data.

3

Methodology

This chapter discusses the various techniques of naturalistic inquiry used in this research: the means by which the sample was selected, the interviewing process, and the analysis of data.

I sought to learn about the factors leading to the success of a sample of African-American male students in a 118-year-old historically black college, Florida Memorial College. I have been a teacher at this college for more than twenty years, and the subject of success factors for the black male became relevant for me when I produced more than a hundred hours of African-American and cross-cultural educational cable television programming for the college. Many of the issues discussed on the program centered on the topic of the "black male in crisis"; yet I knew that black males do succeed. Therefore, the focus of this study was to unearth the supportive factors for success.

Another factor within naturalistic inquiry or ethnographic research which directly relates to my circumstances at the college was my immersion "in the everyday life of the culture being studied." During my long tenure at the college, I have attended traditional events of the school innumerable times: graduation ceremonies, Black History Month celebrations, Donation Day festivities, Founder's Day activities, and several presidential inaugurations. I have also been the chairperson of many college committees, such as the Planning and Development Committee, the Media Committee, and the Tenure Committee, and have served as a faculty member on various other standing and ad hoc committees.

My perceptions and impressions throughout the years became an integral part of this study. For example, I became aware of the spirituality and sense of cooperation and unity within the black culture. I also became aware of the faculty's concern for and nurturing of the students.

In keeping with the axioms of phenomenology, I sought to integrate relevant historical and cultural information in order to give a backdrop for understanding the phenomena discovered. Only within the boundaries of the culture itself would the emerging themes have meaning. For example, only individuals who have knowledge of and insight into the African-American culture and its integral components would discern the emerging themes, such as "nurturing," "bonding," "caring," "choices," and "survival skills" as they relate to the black male. These themes emerged through constant exegesis and analysis of the interviews. As an English teacher, I felt proficient in the process of analysis. Shiva's Circle reflects the process: a circular action of probing the text for the essence of meaning.

THE SETTING

The setting for this study is a historically black college founded in 1879. As discussed in Chapter 2, historically black institutions were founded after the Civil War to give the freed slaves an opportunity for a vocational education. Florida Memorial College is a private, coeducational, Baptist-related college, established by members of the Bethlehem Baptist Association for the training of African-American children. The college was first located in Live Oak, Florida, on the banks of the Suwanee River. In 1918 the academy was relocated to St. Augustine, and in 1968 it was relocated again, from St. Augustine to Miami, due in part to the heightened racial tensions in St. Augustine.

The institution became a four-year college in 1945. Florida Memorial College is a degree-granting institution and offers programs of liberal and technical education. The college has seven academic divisions: the General College, Airway and Computer Sciences, Business Administration, Education and Humanities, Life Long Learning, Natural Sciences and Mathematics, and Social Sciences. The General College is a non-degree-granting entity that monitors the progress of all freshman and sophomore students from their admission through their successful passing of the College-Level Academic Skills Test (CLAST)—a basic skills test in reading, language skills, essay writing, and mathematics decreed by the state of Florida. The other six divisions of the college are degree-granting.

Florida Memorial College serves a culturally diverse student body. During the time of this study, the demographics of the student population analyzed by the Office of Institutional Research showed that students come from various locations in the United States, such as Florida, Illinois, Michigan, New York, New Jersey, Maryland, Connecticut, and California. Many students enrolled at the college also come from other countries, such as the Bahamas, Jamaica, Cuba, Haiti, Saudi Arabia, Colombia, Jordan, and Ghana.

The main campus of Florida Memorial College is situated on a seventy-seven-acre site in a suburban, lower-middle to middle-class neighborhood. The homes in the vicinity of the college are well-maintained family dwellings, and one sees children playing outdoors. Nonetheless, the windows of many of the homes have been secured with iron bars.

The campus is composed of fifteen major facilities. A prominent structure is the religious center, which is located directly across the street from the entrance to the college. It houses a chapel with seating for six hundred people. The center also includes a classroom area for the study of religion and philosophy, as well as offices of the college minister and other religion and philosophy faculty.

The campus site itself is enclosed by an iron fence. Upon entering the campus one drives beneath a black iron arch with the word "Excellence" spanning the entrance gate. To the left of the entrance is a gatehouse, where a security person checks everyone who enters the campus and keeps a record of those who are not members of the college community. From the entrance route, one can see almost the entire circumference of the campus and several of its structures. On the left side of the entrance are four dormitories (two male and two female), housing approximately eight hundred students. When the students are not in the classroom, they frequently congregate in the courtyard of the dormitories; passing by the residence halls one can hear a broad spectrum of musical sounds, ranging from hip hop to reggae to rhythm and blues. One can also see students crowding around a friend's car, conversing and, it appears, enjoying each other's company. Within this same courtyard area are two tennis courts.

The library sits at the midpoint of the campus facing the entrance to the college. In front of the library stands a granite monument listing the names of past Florida Memorial College presidents and their tenures. This prominent monument was presented to the college by the 1991 graduation class. On the south side of the campus across the road from the Opa Locka Airport stands the control tower of the William Lehman Aviation Center and the J. C. Sams Activities Center, which houses the school's cafeteria, the bookstore, and the offices of the Student Government Association. A covered walkway connects the library, the Classroom Building, the Teaching Auditorium, and the Science Building. A lake adjacent to the library, palm trees, and manicured lawns give the campus a tropical appearance. On the right side of the entrance, next to the library, is the Administration Building. To the far right side of the campus, parallel to the Administration Building, are other organizational offices housed in the Student Educational Service Center. Other edifices are the Fine Arts Building and the A. Chester Robinson Athletic Center, which has a floor space of 120 by 90 feet for basketball, volleyball, and other indoor sports. Adjoining the gymnasium is an L-shaped swimming pool, 80 by 53 by 77 feet, for instruction and recreation. All the buildings are clustered within a five-minute walk from any point on the campus. Most of the buildings are one-story structures; the exceptions are the men's residence hall, which has three floors; the aviation building, which has three floors plus a tower; and the library, science, and classroom buildings, all of which have two floors. Except for the administrative offices, the activities center, and the residence halls, all the buildings house classrooms and faculty offices. Parking lots for faculty and students are in front of each building.

THE SAMPLE

The first step in developing the project was to select the sample. As this was a qualitative study, I needed a sample of at least twelve students (Lincoln and Guba, 1985). My thoughts turned to various groups on the campus who, I judged, might meet the criteria as set forth by this study; however, I learned that many groups did not require for membership a grade point average of 3.0, which was one of my criteria. I then contemplated asking divisional chairpersons to recommend their highest-achieving students. Intuitively, however, I felt that the students recommended by the chairpersons might not meet the criteria for leadership on the campus and involvement in the community. My thoughts kept returning to a group of male students, The President's Men. I decided to meet with the program director, Roscoe Warren, to learn about its criteria. He stated that members had to have a 3.0 grade-point average upon entering the program and had to express interest in campus and community involvement. This excited me, as it matched the criteria that I established for my project. I gave Mr. Warren a copy of my proposal, which indicated my intention to interview African-American male students and included the research questions. After reading my proposal and discussing the project with me, he gave his consent to interview the students in the organization. He introduced the project to the group at its next meeting and asked me to attend an awards banquet in which some of the students in the program were to receive athletic awards. He felt that in this way I could meet the nucleus of the organization. I attended the banquet, met the students, and discussed the project with them. I was informed that there were seventeen African-American students in the organization, more than enough to satisfy the requirement for a qualitative study. The members were very receptive. I asked them for their local telephone numbers so that I could contact them to set up interviews.

At designated times, the students came into my office at the college to fill out a consent form and a biographical profile form for background data on themselves and their family. The biographical profile was implemented in order to supplement the interviews as well as to corroborate data collected from the interviews. This was the first step in triangulation. During this meeting, the students spent one or more hours with me in an interviewing session. The interviewing process, the transcribing of the tapes, and the "cut and paste" procedure of categorizing the data from the interviews required two semesters to complete, the fall of 1993 and the spring of 1994. Throughout this process I reflected on the students' answers to the interview questions and examined the transcriptions to become familiar with the findings and to discover emerging themes.

The purpose of The President's Men, from which the sample of students used for this study came, was to develop a nucleus of capable student leaders to serve as mentors, role models, tutors, and peer counselors at this historically black college. They were a support system not only to each other but also to other students on the campus. In addition, the students acted as representatives or ambassadors of the college at major events, such as graduation, Donation Day, Founder's Day, concerts given in honor of the president of the college, and community activities. Members of the program also addressed middle school and high school students, sharing with them their own personal experiences and imploring them to take their education seriously, to finish high school, and go on to a college education.

The criteria for being invited to join The President's Men were a 3.0 grade-point average, leadership potential, community and campus involvement, recommendations from the faculty and members of the administrative staff, and willingness to remain in the program for the duration of my study or until graduation, whichever occurred first. Students who qualified to participate in The President's Men's program had to be approved by an officer of the college and then interviewed by members of the program who were also members of the student cabinet; these students gave final approval or refusal.

The black male student population of the college at the time of the study (1995) totaled 597. Of that number, 537 students (90 percent) had been born inside the United States, and sixty students (10 percent) were born elsewhere. In The President's Men, were a total of thirty-four members of whom seventeen were African American; the remaining seventeen members had been born outside the United States. This represented a disproportionate number of students in the organization not born inside of the United States to students who were African American. I asked the director of the program (who was an officer of the college) his view as to what caused this disproportionate make-up, and as to why, considering the demographics of the total male population in the school, there were not more African Americans in The President's Men. He explained that the organization was voluntary in nature and that although the students were selected by the criteria outlined above, students had to fill out an application form and return it to the director's office, and exhibit interest. Taking the initiative to become a member was an important part of the membership process. Apparently, the students born outside of the United States were highly motivated to take that initiative.

It was apparent that the African-American students in The President's Men represented the highest caliber of male African-American students in the college. Therefore, for the purpose of the study, I divided the African Americans and the black male students born outside the United States into separate groups—Cluster I (African Americans) and Cluster II (students born outside the United States).

THE INTERVIEWING PROCESS

In this study, all thirty-four students in the organization were interviewed using a prepared list of seven research questions. Patton (1987) referred to this type of interviewing as "the general interview guide approach . . . [which] serves as a basic checklist during the interview to make sure that all relevant topics are covered" (p. 109, p. 111). He stated that this approach should not inhibit the interviewer from asking additional questions; the researcher should feel free to use a conversational style, to act spontaneously, and to explore issues that emerge, in keeping with the holistic aspect of qualitative research (p. 111).

The seven research questions framed the study, and a conversational approach was used. At the beginning of the interviewing session, the researcher introduced the participants into the project by discussing the overall study. In this way, the students were also being taught about scholarly research. They affirmed the need for this type of study and felt they were a part of something important. They wanted to share their views on success factors as well as on the obstacles that they had to overcome in order to achieve their goals.

Minority groups often go unheard; consequently, qualitative research is best suited, as it reveals and investigates the inner person. I asked each student initially the seven research questions and then asked follow-up questions. Finally, four more questions emerged as relevant to understanding the background or inner feelings of the student. These questions are referred to in the study as "key questions" (KQ). As noted above, the students were also requested to fill out a biographical profile form, which added to the data collected.

The average interview, when transcribed, was ten pages long, single-spaced. The compiled interviews comprised 358 pages. An Olympus Pearlcorder L400 micro-cassette recorder was used to tape the interviews; an Olympus Pearlcorder T1010 transcriber was used to transcribe them.

The students never appeared apprehensive in answering the questions posed. They wanted to share their experiences. They were serious and focused on giving information. All the information was verified by the director of The President's Men's program. He knew the participants on a personal level and had dialogues with individual members of the group, as well as dialogues in group seminar settings, regarding their personal activities and any stumbling blocks that they were experiencing. These open discussions led to a sharing of experiences and to mutual support within the group.

TRUSTWORTHINESS CRITERIA

Lincoln and Guba (1985) listed three activities that increase the probability of reliable findings and interpretations in naturalistic inquiry: prolonged engagement, persistent observation, and triangulation (p. 301). As the researcher in this study on "success factors," I have met the criteria for prolonged engagement and persistent observation, having been immersed in the college culture since 1971 as assistant professor of English and then in 1987 as associate professor of English. My present title is professor of Higher Education. In my professional capacity during my twenty-six years teaching at this college, I have taught the entire program of literature being offered by the English department, from the classics to the contem-porary period, in all genres. This also includes the teachings of black leaders of the past, such as Frederick Douglass, Booker T. Washington, and W.E.B. DuBois. It is relevant to note that the themes that emerged in this study were similar to those that had emerged from the writings of these seminal figures: the spiritual aspect at the core of their being, and determination to become educated.

TRIANGULATION

The issue of triangulation has been met in several different ways. First, each transcribed interview was read by the respondent, who signed a verification letter deeming the interview "true" and "correct." (In qualitative research this is referred to as "member checks" [Lincoln and Guba, p. 314].) Also, the findings and analysis of the study were made available in the office of the director of The President's Men to give the respondents the opportunity to read the contents and to give feedback. The process was completely confidential. The students did not read each other's interviews.

Selected colleagues at the college who were in positions to give reliable feedback and recommendations also reviewed the data, as well as the findings. In qualitative research, these individuals would fall into the category of "key informants" and "peer debriefers." Crabtree and Miller (1992) defined "key informants" as "individuals who possess special knowledge, status, or communication skills, who are willing to share their knowledge and skills" (p. 75). Lincoln and Guba (1985) emphasized the relevance of "peer debriefer," asserting that it is a useful technique in establishing credibility: "All questions are in order during a debriefing, whether they pertain to substantive, methodological, legal, ethical, or any other relevant matters" (p. 308).

The following individuals were asked to serve in this capacity as key informants and peer debriefers:

The director of The President's Men, Roscoe Warren, examined the biographical profile forms to ascertain if there was a need to check respondents' college records for any apparent discrepancies in the students' written statements. His position at the college was Director of Enrollment and Management; he was also at the time vice mayor of the city of Homestead, Florida.

The chairperson of the Division of Social Sciences, Dr. Sandra T. Thompson, was a constant and faithful mentor for the study from the onset, verifying that the themes that emerged were in fact components of African-American culture. In addition, she provided feedback within her academic field of sociology.

Associate Professor of Music Charles C. Clency contributed his time and expertise by providing a historical perspective on the Negro spiritual as it evolved in American culture from the time of slavery.

Assistant Professor of History C. Anthony Fraser, a native of Jamaica, gave feedback particularly as related to Cluster II students, those born outside the United States, the majority of whom were raised in the Caribbean.

Assistant Professor of Art Alvin L. Pondexter lent his perceptions to the description of the physical setting of the college.

Vincent Ashley, a 1989 graduate of the college and at the time of my research a counselor there, acted in the above-mentioned roles. He was close enough in age, at twenty-seven, to the respondents to be a contemporary of theirs, yet as a graduate and as a professional on the campus he was "removed" from them. He provided valuable insight into the "obstacles" that the respondents had to surmount and the determination that was needed on a daily basis to overcome these obstacles.

The above-cited individuals were chosen to take roles in the study because they were thought to have the experience and professional insight to probe the findings for inaccurate statements or themes that did not seem credible. These individuals served as "key informants," and "peer debriefers," because racially and ethnically they "stood in the shoes" of the individuals being studied.

TRANSFERABILITY OF THE STUDY

In naturalistic inquiry, only a potential applier of the assumptions generated would know if the information is applicable to his or her site. Lincoln and Guba (1985) asserted that "it is not the naturalist's task to provide an index of transferability; it is her or his responsibility to provide the data base that makes transferability judgments possible on the part of potential appliers" (p. 316). In this study, the demographic information, the "portraits" of the students that emerged from the quoted material, and the description of the college setting fulfilled the requirement for "rich" description.

DATA ANALYSIS

The analysis of this study was guided by the editing style set forth by Crabtree and Miller (1992):

This style is termed "editing" because the interpreter enters the text much like an editor searching for meaningful segments, cutting, pasting, and rearranging until the reduced summary reveals the interpretive truth in the text. (p. 20)

The editing style is consistent with the multimethod approach used in this study: ethnography, phenomenology, hermeneutics, and grounded theory: It "moves analysis closer to the subjective/interpretive side of the analysis continuum" (Crabtree and Miller, p. 20).

The first step in "editing" was to separate a transcribed interview and all other data pertaining to the respondent into individual files, using numbers in place of the students' name, to maintain anonymity. The files (thirty-four) were number-coded according to the order that the respondents were interviewed. The individual files were then placed into two groupings, referred to as Cluster I and Cluster II. Throughout the study, the Cluster I and Cluster II files were kept separate.

RESEARCH QUESTIONS

The next step was to arrange and reduce the data for simpler readability across the sample. Accordingly, the study was divided into units; one unit for each of the original seven research questions and the four additional questions (referred to as "key" questions) that had been added to the study as it evolved. The seven research questions that guided the study were:

Figure 3.1
Editing Analysis Style

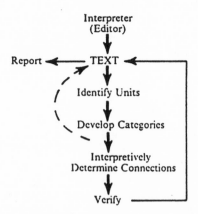

Source: From *Doing Qualitative Research* by B. Crabtree and W. L. Miller (1992), Newbury Park, CA: Sage.

1. What factors did you identify as contributing to your success?
2. What factors did you identify as obstacles to your success?
3. What courses of action have you taken to overcome the obstacles that you had encountered?
4. Who/what were the major influences in your life: family, teachers, peers, athletics, church, role models?
5. What activities and organizations did you identify as being important to your development?
6. What were the reasons why these activities and organizations are important to you?
7. What recommendations did you have for younger black males?

The four "key" questions that were added as the study progressed:

1. What thoughts passed through your mind when making a decision?
2. Describe the home that you grew up in.
3. What is inside you that motivated you to succeed?
4. How do you define success?

The responses to each question were indexed in lists, by a cut-and-paste method on a word processor. In this way, emerging categories could be identified. For example, for Research Question no. 1 ("What factors did you identify as contributing to your success?") a relevant category emerged: *mother/grandmother*, the primary caretaker.

CATEGORIES OF THE STUDY

Diverse categories emerged from the responses to the questions, as well as from the general content of the interviews. These categories could be further explained by "key" words and their "connections." An example of a category that emerged was *major influences*; one of the major influences in the students' lives was "family"; the "connections" or "linkages" to the "key" word, *family*, were "brothers, sisters, aunts, uncles, and cousins." Another example of a *major influence* in the students' lives was *role models*. The connections or linkages to the key word *role models* were "mentors," "teachers," and "coaches." Consequently, all quotations containing these "key" words, and their connecting terms, were indexed in lists, by a cut-and-paste method on a word processor.

To further illustrate the editing process, another major category defined in the study was *danger*. The "key" word designation was *streets*; its linking terms were "violence," "drugs," "gangs," and "crime."

The theme of "survival" emerged from studying the quotations that included these terms:

We go outside where we were right in front of the house and play football, and just play out in the little parking area that they had, so most of the time was spent in the home to try and get through the *violence* that was outside. I kept safe from that mainly through common sense, as I said, because most kids have common sense, but they don't use it. I was able to look, at a very young age, and see that if I took *drugs*, or something, I saw what it did to J, then I knew that could happen to me, and, basically, through common sense, and through my family constantly talking to me, constantly being with me, I survived. I really did.

CODING PROCEDURE

When a quotation was excerpted from an interview, the quotation was coded according to file number, page number, and paragraph number. (The code "Int.3.1.4" referred to interview 3, page 1, paragraph 4 of the transcribed interview.) This created an easy retrieval system from the list(s) to the student's interview.

The coding procedure used to classify the data was as follows. The seven research questions were coded RQ1, RQ2, RQ3, RQ4, RQ5, RQ6, and RQ7. As other pertinent "key" questions evolved, they were coded KQ1, KQ2, KQ3, and KQ4. Finally, an example of a category code (designating the category mentioned above for "Major Influences," specifically "Role Model," with linkages of "mentors," "teachers," and "coaches") is "CAT:MAJ.INFL/RM:m/t/c."

After studying the listed quotations, I established a new document, "Analysis and Significance of the Research." Emerging themes grounded in the data were then ascertained. In the margin of this document next to the students' quoted remarks handwritten notes and memos were appended, the result of constant reflection and deliberation. For example, for Research Question no. 3 ("Courses of action to overcome obstacles") themes that emerged were "analyzing the situation," "observation," "listening," "action-oriented responses," and "belief in self." The handwritten notes and memos in the margin, associated in qualitative research with the "constant comparative method," gave recommendations to explore further the concept of "choices," which surfaced within the context of the quotations. The persistent reflection and deliberation on the themes and concepts that emerged from the data were in keeping with Crabtree's and Miller's (1992) explanation of "spiraling around the hermeneutic circle . . . from understanding to interpretation to deeper understanding to more comprehensive interpretation."

DOCUMENTING THE THEMES

When the quotations began to overlap, it was felt that the material was exhausted; the dissecting of the interviews came to an end, and it was time to document the themes that emerged from the data. Consequently, a theme sheet was developed: "Themes That Emerged from Units and Categories in the Study on Success Factors, Theme Sheet I." Themes from the document "Analysis and Significance of the Research," previously described, were listed. Through additional analysis of the listed themes, now separated and clearly noted in a five-page draft, insights were derived and written down in the form of jottings and memos within the text of Theme Sheet I. Overlapping themes became apparent.

Therefore, the next step was to integrate as many themes as possible. The result was Theme Sheet 2, which contained four themes: *bonding, caring, choices*, and *survival skills*. From careful deliberation of the data, an overriding concept emerged: that in order for the African-American male child to succeed, he needed the positive influence of being *nurtured*.

SAS was used to collate the demographics from the biographical profile form. SAS refers to a statistical analysis system formerly used by the University of Miami.

4

Emergent Findings and Postreview of the Literature

This chapter is organized by addressing significant themes that have emerged from interviewing the African-American students in this study and also the relevant literature which supports these findings; achievement motivation in cross-cultural literature; and distinctions between African-American students and those born outside the United States.

The theme of being *bonded* to someone or something when growing up emerged in the interviews of these African-American students as an important element in keeping the respondent "on track." Examples were the bond between mother and son, the link to religion, the link to family, and the link to a caring mentor or role model. These themes, along with students' quotations and a postreview of the literature, are examined and discussed.

THE BOND BETWEEN MOTHER AND SON

The major bonding of the respondents in the study was with their mother or grandmother, or both, if no father was in the home. The respondents recalled that their mothers had set a positive example for them while they were growing up. Both mother and grandmother had "molded" the young men and were their "backbone," that which held them up.

With my mom's determination, as far as when I look at the past with my mom, my mom didn't graduate from high school. She just completed up to her senior year, and really all her life has basically been work, work, work, work, work, for the family. . . . It's been motivating for me, although she pushes us. She would make sure we cannot come in her house without a high school diploma. . . . It's just her integrity, her determination, her perseverance, and her character.

* * *

My mother, of course. . . . She's always telling me that she wants me to have better than what she had . . . by just supporting me in whatever I do, just standing behind me always . . . just being a typical mother . . . just wanting the best for her son. . . . My grandmother is also like a mother to me. They are like my mother and father. Both of them are [my] the backbone of CL.

* * *

I guess growing up with a single parent, mother paralyzed, income under $10,000, you had to become bonded as one, and I guess, right today, we as one, we love each other, so I guess that's the role that they [family] played in my life.

* * *

Well, I contribute my success to mainly my grandmother and my mother, because they kept me—I could have been doing a lot of other things, bad things, but they kept me in the church, and kept me busy with Optimist football and basketball . . . I didn't want to let my mother down, and I didn't want to let my grandmother down.

These are illustrations of the mother or grandmother, or both, as examples; they are the conduit through which the son learns and is guided through adolescence.

King and Mitchell (1990) stated that there is a scarcity of scholarly research on how black mothers raise sons. Therefore, they designed a qualitative study that examined parenting from two sources: a semi-structured group interview with five African-American mothers (and the two researchers, who are also African-American mothers), and an examination of mother-to-son relationships in African-American literature. Their aim was to determine if the literature reflected the lived experience, based on the premise that art mirrors life. Their study did in fact find that the fictional mothers mirrored the "real life" mothers.

The authors' comparisons of African-American literature with real-life situations is useful in this study on success factors, as it supports two emergent findings: first, that the mother (or grandmother, or both) is the primary person in the son's life and that this primary caretaker sets examples for "hard work" and "perseverance"; second, that the mother (and/or grandmother) is very concerned about the survival of her son in the unsafe environment in which they live, which becomes a constant worry when raising her son.

King and Mitchell (1990) argued that the mother is the major bond and that African-American literature reflects "the mother who is the link to, the filter through which knowledge comes and the rite of passage is initiated" (p. 26). King and Mitchell illustrated the hypothesis that the black mother teaches by being an example to her child with a poem, "Mother to Son," by Langston Hughes.

> Well, son, I'll tell you:
> Life for me ain't been no crystal stair.
> It's had tacks in it,
> And splinters,

And boards torn up,
And places with no carpet on the floor—
Bare.
But all the time
I'se been a-climbin' on,
And reachin' landin's,
And turnin' corners,
And sometimes goin' in the dark
Where there ain't been no light.
So boy, don't you turn back.
Don't you set down on the steps
'Cause you finds it's kinder hard.
Don't you fall now—
For I'se still goin', honey,
I'se still climbin',
And life for me ain't been no crystal stair.

Analyzing the poem, the researchers observed that the "mother teaches by example and by word" and that the poem shows "work-worn women" who evoke images of life's hardships yet strive despite the obstacles and continue to climb. The lines "And sometimes goin' in the dark / Where there ain't been no light" are an example of "spiritual and physical endurance." The refrain, "Life for me ain't been no crystal stair," reflects the theme of "pain and perseverance" and the ability to cope (p. 28). The themes of life's hardships, of striving, of spirituality, and endurance are strands throughout this study of factors contributing to the success of black male students.

King and Mitchell (1990), in discussing the issue of survival, stated that this important issue "has not been explored in other investigations of black parenting." They mentioned Forcey (1987), who "identifies survival as a central concern of black mothers of sons but fails to analyze or interpret its significance" (p. 3). Forcey (1987), in a section called "Voices from Mothers," quoted a black welfare mother of two sons, aged twenty-four and twenty-six: "They've got to be taught how to survive. That is what I've been trying to get across to them for the past twenty some odd years. That is what motherhood is all about in my opinion" (p. 47). To justify their claim that black mothers "prepare their sons to survive in a hostile environment" (p. 12), King and Mitchell cited Richard Wright's autobiography, *Black Boy*, referring to strong admonitions by Wright's mother to her son on how to survive:

"Take this money, this note, and this stick," she said. "Go to the store and buy those groceries. If those boys bother you, then fight." I was baffled. My mother was telling me to fight, a thing I had never done before. . . . "Please, let me wait until tomorrow," I begged. "No," she said, "go now! If you come back into this house without those groceries, I'll whip you!" She slammed the door, and I heard the key turn in the lock. . . . I had the choice of being beaten at home or away from home. . . . If I were beaten at home, there was absolutely nothing I could do about it; but if I were beaten in the streets, I had a chance to fight and defend myself. I walked slowly down the sidewalk, coming closer to the gang of boys. (Wright, pp. 24–25)

The authors explained that in *Black Boy* "Mrs. Wright has neither the time nor inclination to explain her admonitions to her son, as is often the case in real life where the immediacy of danger is ever-present" (p. 13).

The feeling of the "immediacy of danger" and the concern about the survival of the child, passed from mother to son, or grandmother to grandson, surfaced as a significant theme in this study:

My mom was like, "Listen, you're going to do this this way, and you're not going to ask all these questions—why or why not—'cause I don't have the answers for you. You just do this this way, and I guarantee you you're going to be all right." She told me different things—to go this way and to go that way, but she never did give me a reason, though I found out the reasons later.

* * *

My mother was my father also. She was there every day. . . . She was strict on me. Very strict—had to be in the house before dark. I couldn't make calls after nine. I had to be in bed before nine. I couldn't watch movies that had the R-rated, X-rated. I couldn't have a girlfriend. I couldn't go out on dates. She treated me like, sometimes, like fathers treat their young daughters. And I couldn't go out on dates until I was about like seventeen years old, something like that. I had to get good grades. If I didn't, she would scold me. There are people that say scolding children is wrong, but, for me, that worked for me, because now I am a very good person. And she [my mother] wanted me to survive and become a great person. She wanted her son, as she tells me, "You're my only son," and she has to keep me. That's mainly why I think she kept me away from trouble, mainly death.

* * *

My mother had me at a very young age, and my grandmother was the type in our home, and even now, she handles everything. She has the business smarts. She has the sense of how to take care of things and do everything; whereas my mother, she was like a young girl who, at the time, made a lot of mistakes and now, you know, she looks back and says, "Oh, I wish I had done this and done that"; but my grandmother, on the other hand, was the type that if she had a chance, she went to school, she did whatever she could do, so, basically, in my household what transpired was more of like learning, being taught, me and my mother both being taught by my grandmother, how to live in this life, and how to survive, and how to make it.

The statements demonstrate why the students listen to and respect their elders. Collins (1991), in "The Meaning of Motherhood in Black Culture," remarked that the power of older black women extends into the community. She quoted an anecdote told to her by her grandmother, one that illustrates that women's control can extend beyond their home into the neighborhood:

One night . . . as Grandmother sat crocheting alone at about two in the morning, a young man walked into the living room carrying the portable TV from upstairs. She said, "Who are you looking for this time of night?" As Grandmother described the incident to me over

the phone, I could hear a tone of voice that I know well. It said, "Nice boys don't do that."
So I imagine the burglar heard his own mother or grandmother at that moment. He joined
in the familial game just created: "Well, he told me that I could borrow it." "Who told you?"
"John." "Um, um, no John lives here. You got the wrong house." (p. 175)

After this exchange, the young man turned around and returned the television to
the bedroom.

Johnson (Johnson and Bennett, 1992) wrote about his mother as the "indomitable mother spirit." At her funeral she was eulogized by historian Lerone Bennett,
Jr. Bennett said she was "one of the last survivors of a select band of strong Black
women who could not be blocked or stopped by anything" (p. 321). He said that
she was like the "tens of thousands of unsung Black mothers and grandmothers
. . . [who] rose above the scourges of [their] environment and testified to the
indomitable tenacity of the human spirit" (p. 321). In this study, the students' words,
and the literature cited in this chapter, communicate this same "indomitable mother
spirit" that Johnson (1992) expressed. If no father is in the home, the students'
mothers and/or grandmothers represent, or are archetypes for "hard work," "integrity," "determination," "perseverance," "strength," and "character." The students'
grandmothers, if they were involved in their upbringing, provided stability and a
positive foundation. Throughout this study, the theme of bonding to a significant
person in the students' lives remained constant.

THE LINK TO RELIGION

Fifteen out of the seventeen students interviewed emphasized their religious-
spiritual orientation, reinforced throughout their lives by their mother, grandmother,
or both.

I believe the greatest person outside of my mother was my grandmother, who somehow saw
something different in me. Also, the greatest institution, I think, that made a really great
impact on my life, beyond a doubt, is the church. My grandmother made sure that I was at
Sunday school and in church every Sunday. She moved my life. . . . She and the church
molded my life at an early age.

*   *   *

At the beginning of my life, it [church] played a significant role, because it taught me the
difference between right and wrong. . . . The first factor would be my mother for introducing
God into my life at a young age. Growing up I thought that my mother was too firm in forcing
me to go to Sunday school, regular service and weekday service, but now I am realizing that
I am reaping the rewards of that association.

*   *   *

I went to church every Sunday. When you're younger, you just go, because your parents
wake you up every Sunday morning, and you just go, and, I mean, of course, I'm sure,
[church] had an influence. It probably instilled values in me that someone . . . who never
attended church, or maybe only went on Easter, whatever the case may be, would not have
had. But, of course, being in a religious environment, and instilling belief in God into a child,

and the way I perceived it in church, and the way I still perceive it—people are still what I consider to be in fear of God, in order to encourage their children to act morally. . . . Religion kind of conforms and keeps people moral, and I think that it played an important role in my younger years.

*   *   *

By me being in the church and listening to my grandmother, you know, patience, believe in God, and be patient, and things will work out; don't go for the fast money, and all that kind of stuff, 'cause it's not gonna last forever, so those were the things I was exposed to.

*   *   *

When [people in the church] see a young person, a young adult going to church on a regular basis, they kinda get interested in what's going on in your life, so after a lot of people got interested in me, to myself, I said, "Well, I can't do anything bad to let them down; I can't do anything bad to let my grandmother down." So, that kinda kept me going. When things got a little rough, that kept me going, knowing that I wouldn't want to see their faces if I was to get in trouble, go to jail, or something like that.

Cheatham and Stewart (1993) referred to the black church as the oldest social institution in African-American history, quoting C. Eric Lincoln that the black church is "the spiritual face of the black community" (p. 43). Littlejohn-Blake and Darling (1993), writing about the strengths of African-American families, observed that there is a strong sense of religious spirituality within black families and that it is "woven into the very fabric of society and is a central characteristic of the African psyche. . . . This system of core beliefs is the foundation of the inner strength of the person" (p. 462).

Billingsley (1992) confirmed that the religious orientation of black families is one of their greatest historical strengths (p. 349) and quoted findings from a national survey of black Americans (1979–80) that "an overwhelming eighty-four percent indicated a belief that religion was very important in their lives when they were growing up" (p. 355).

Billingsley also quoted from a study entitled "Black Initiative and Governmental Responsibility: An Essay by the Committee on Policy for Racial Justice" (1989):

Blacks have always embraced the central values of the society, augmented those values in response to the unique experiences of slavery and subordination, incorporated them into a strong religious tradition, and espoused them fervently and persistently. (p. 72)

DuBois (1961) confirmed "that the Negro church antedates the Negro home . . . [which] leads us to regard this institution as peculiarly the expression of the inner ethical life of a people in a sense seldom true elsewhere" (p. 499). In present-day practice, the church can be seen as a facsimile of the family. From the perspective of those who are affiliated with the church, "the pastor functions as male parent. The pastor's wife . . . functions as female parent. The governing board of deacons, elders, or presbyters functions as the older siblings" (Cheatham and Steward, pp. 36, 37). Conceptualizing the black church as an important entity within the life of the black community, Cheatham and Steward (1993) evoked E. F. Frazier's image that the black church is "a nation within a nation" (p. 36).

In a study entitled *Family Life and School Achievement: Why Poor Black Children Succeed or Fail*, Clark (1983) noted:

In low-income families a key factor in the educational success of a child may be a strong parental religious-spiritual orientation. A mother who directs her children toward moral values in society, while strenuously curtailing their contact with potentially negative influences, can usually obtain the children's respect. As this respect is attained, it is possible for the mother to effect a strong educational orientation in her child. It is particularly important that the child learn the appropriate values at an early age so that the child's value orientation may become a way of life. (p. 62)

Furthermore, as H. P. McAdoo (1988) asserted, "that which should emerge from parent-child interaction is a sense of Supreme Being[;] . . . that it is important that African American children engage in the religious ritual[;] . . . [that they] understand, respect, and obey the supreme spirit which makes them human . . . a power and a will that is greater than all else. . . . Therefore, help them to realize there are no limitations" (p. 51).

The historic religious tradition of the African American has its roots in the experience of slavery. During slavery, religious practices were analogous to the legacy of the ancient bards, who passed down through oral tradition the folk wisdom of a people. As in ancient cultures, religious hymns and plaintive cries of the slaves unified, bonded, and offered a catharsis for the group. The African Americans' ability to endure was in part due to their religious orientation. In examining the students' responses, it became apparent that religion is an important support system and bond in students' lives; the church still serves as the means by which black culture is transmitted to African Americans.

THE LINK TO FAMILY

The theme that emerged in this study regarding family was that "while parents may or may not have been 'on their case,'" other members of the family were a support system, older brothers and sisters were often role models, and siblings, some of whom did not fare well themselves, kept the respondents "in line" (Bowser and Perkins, 1991, p. 186). Also, other members of the family, such as grandfathers, grandmothers, aunts, or uncles, verbally reinforced maternal measures for the protection of the child. The study showed that members of the family cared for, guided, and instructed the respondents and that the respondents listened to the advice and were influenced by it, as the following comments demonstrate:

Everybody was getting into gangs, and, because my brother did not get into gangs, and my sister always told my brother never to get involved with guys in gangs, I never got involved with them either. So, I just followed the path. My brother didn't do it, so I didn't do it. . . .

When my brother told me something, or my sister told me something, because they're older than I, I just took that for being the truth.

* * *

Well, my sister was more of the type where she would understand where I was coming from, and my older brother would say, "OK, listen, I understand your problems that you're having, but the fact remains that you have to still stick with your books. No matter what, everything else is gonna come and go, but your education is always gonna be there." So, he would really stay on me about books.

* * *

My mother, my brothers and family were contributing factors to whatever I will be, or whatever I am now. . . . I had brothers that the community admired, because they weren't in trouble. . . . I was the youngest of seven brothers, and the brother next to me is like five years [older], so I was a lot smaller than everybody else, so I never tried to challenge my brothers. . . . I had one brother that kinda stayed a little bit in trouble, but he, for some reason, if he saw me trying to get in trouble, he was just like he was a monk, and I had to be "purified." I had to go wash my hands, and everything I had to correct, so I applaud him for that.

* * *

My grandmother lived with us. She had a lot to do with my upbringing, because when my parents was away, at work, she would always be home, and she would be the first person I would see when I came home from school, during elementary, junior high, and high school . . . and she would always listen to me, and, usually I would tell her a lot about my problems and she would understand with no problem, because grandmothers are like that. She was always there for me and she had a lot to do with our upbringing.

In "Success against the Odds: Young Black Men Tell What It Takes," Bowser and Perkins (1991) recorded findings from a qualitative study designed to gain knowledge about factors underlying the academic success of forty minority black and Hispanic high school students, both male and female, virtually all of whom came from working-class homes and half of whom had single parents. Of the forty students, approximately half were black males. The students selected for the sample had 3.0-plus grade-point averages, and they had previously attended segregated junior high schools. When the study took place, they were in highly competitive college preparatory tracks in three integrated suburban high schools in California. Although the researchers were primarily interested in "success against the odds" for young black male students, as indicated by the title of their research, the group of minority students that they interviewed cut across all categories; the individuals in the sample had been identified by district principals. Because of the "mix" of culture and gender, the researchers felt the study "represented a unique opportunity to derive insight on what makes for academic success for working-class minority students" (p. 184).

The relevance of Bowser's and Perkins's study to this study is that the findings correspond. Parallel findings are that

the key persons, who they named as their main sources of family support for high academic achievement, consisted of grandparents or, more often, older brothers or sisters. While parents may or may not have been "on their case" and were pleased that the student was doing well, it was actually some other member of the family who helped the student to define his long-term goals and who turned him on to high academic achievement. (p. 186)

It is significant that although the siblings of these students motivated them to excel, the siblings themselves did not achieve in school and that

these older brothers and sisters had made all sorts of mistakes, primary of which was failure in school . . . [resulting in] troubled lives, purposelessness, underemployment. . . . It turns out that the experiences of these older brothers and sisters serve as a powerful source of motivation to take some other route . . . [nevertheless], these older siblings became directly involved in making certain that their younger brother or sister did not end up as they did. (p. 186)

EXTENDED KINSHIP RELATIONSHIPS

Cheatham and Stewart (1993) pointed out that "female-headed households survive in the black community because of the cultural tradition of extended kinship relationships . . . and strong kinship bonds as manifested in the capacity to absorb other individuals into the family structure . . . [and because of the] flexibility of family members' roles and . . . religious orientation" (p. 332). The "kinship bond" is significantly illustrated by one of the students in this study, whose aunt took him from a foster home when he was six years old:

At six years old, I was taken [from a foster home] by my aunt, and from then on, I stayed in Liberty City in the projects. . . . My aunt, she raised seven of us. She had her own four children that she raised along with me, my little brother, and my little sister. . . . My aunt, she is a religious person, very religious. And she stands firm in her beliefs. She was strong, and she proved that by raising seven of us as a single parent. . . . I had good support from my aunt and family. . . . My aunt, my family—they influenced me.

Green (1991) cited a study by Johnson et al. (1988) that investigated one-parent homes headed by females to discover if they hindered a child's achievement. The population for the study was low-income minority youth: 80 percent African American, 12 percent Hispanic, and 4 percent Native Americans and Asians (overall 44 percent female and 56 percent male). They found that the academic success of youths from one-parent homes was not impeded: "It is not the number of parents, but the level of parental expectations regarding academic achievement that is the determining factor in the educational achievement of African-American youth" (pp. 6–7).

In "The Meaning of Motherhood in Black Culture," Collins (1991) emphasized that the central importance of motherhood in black culture has its roots in African societies. She asserted that the image of motherhood is at the core of all rituals in West African societies. The "biological mother/child bond is valued, [but] child care was a collective responsibility, a situation fostering . . . woman-centered 'mothering' networks" (p. 171). Collins also noted that current research shows that "mothering networks" still exist within the black culture in this country. Throughout this study, the "mother figure"—whether the biological mother, the grandmother, or another significant individual, such as an aunt—surfaced, giving credence to the major role that the mother or "mother figure" continues to play in black culture.

Before leaving the "Link to Family" and "Extended Kinship Relationships," it is important to recount the findings of H. P. McAdoo (1988) that

> African American parent-child interactions were characterized by an atmosphere or attitude that emphasized strong family ties, unconditional love, respect for self and others, and the assumed natural goodness of the child. . . . Child-rearing techniques associated with the parent-child bond centered on the unconditional expression of love[;] even though a parent expressed anger, meted out punishment and showed disappointment, it never canceled out the love associated with the parental-child bond. (p. 49)

When the students in this study were asked to describe the homes that they had grown up in, the themes that emerged were not material possessions but that the homes "within" were full of love, had family unity, and were "close knit":

> It was a small home. It was full of love, full of joy; we had a sense of family unity. Much, much respect—that was one thing that my parents and grandmother stressed; respect your elders and respect each other and love each as sisters and brothers.

* * *

> I came from a family that looked after one another, being that I am the youngest child, I had my older brothers and sisters that watched out over me; I played every kind of sport, and my family came out to watch me play, so they provided the support system early-on in my life that I would need to feel good about myself.

* * *

> It was a lot of discipline, and most of the time when I was growing up my mom was in college, and my grandmother really kinda raised me and was like the father figure to me, so it was okay, but, even though there was no male in the home, I still felt that they did a good job in bringing me up, because they kept me active in a lot of things to keep me busy. I think they did a pretty good job.

* * *

> The house that I grew up in had a lot of love. There were only two women in the house, and I was the only young man in the house, and sometimes it would be a little rough not having a father image in the household, but in that house, those two women reared a young man that has a lot of love on the inside of him.

FATHER'S ROLE IN THE HOME

The seventeen interviews with students in Cluster I (African-American students) revealed that seven fathers lived in the home. From the respondents' answers, the fathers that lived in the home provided stability and were role models to the respondents, being strong and emphatic in their teachings and influential in their lives:

His ultimate rule was—you go to school and get an education. . . . He never would allow us to stand on corners. . . . We had to be inside a certain time. . . . [Asked about his role model, respondent said:] My father . . . the hero, was always the man who had to go out and put food on the table.

* * *

My father . . . provided me with the things that I needed to be as successful as possible, and I try to take advantage of it. My father is a Supervisor at Atlantic Steel. . . . He has been there for about twenty-five years.

* * *

My father was an influence in my life. . . . My father first got me in playing football. . . . My father was employed by the Sheriff's Department . . . as a deputy sheriff. . . . My father is my role model.

* * *

My father, he stayed on my case; he worked at Sears for twenty something years; my father was the biggest role model in my life, just being a man in today's society and being able to make it without doing wrong.

Walter R. Allen, in "Race, Income and Family Dynamics: A Study of Adolescent Male Socialization Processes and Outcomes," supported the suggestion in the above-stated quotations that when black fathers are in the home, they are "active in childcare and socialization, and sharing warm, close personal relationships with their sons. . . . The mother's central role in the family was not taken as a negation of the father's role, rather, it was seen as complementing the father's role" (Spencer, Brookins, and Allen, p. 291).

J. L. and J. B. McAdoo (1994) observed that . . . economically sufficient [black] fathers were warm and loving toward their children . . . their verbal and nonverbal interactions with their children were observed as nurturant. . . . When they reprimanded their children, they would provide explanations regarding the unacceptable behavior and sometimes express their expectations about future child behaviors. (Majors and Gordon, p. 293)

THE ABSENT FATHER

The respondents who did not have a father in the home expressed a need for a father:

It was like he always came around at the right time. When it seemed like I was down and out and tired . . . he would take me for three or four days and talk to me . . . man to man talks. . . . That's how I got my perception on life. . . . I would just sit down and just realize things.

* * *

I needed a father around. . . . I was a terrific athlete, and, I guess, in a way, my brother played that daddy role, because he was always there for me, every wrestling match he was there, every football game, so, basically, I wish I did have a father, but my brother played that role, and I have to live with it.

* * *

When I was young, I needed a father role, but he was absent. . . . At this point in my life, I don't really need a father, but he wasn't there for me when I was young.

*   *   *

Sometimes, it would be a little rough not having a father image in the household. . . . My father is incarcerated, and he's in prison now. . . . It's amazing to know that you can grow up without a father. . . . I missed that love from a man's point of view, having the male figure in the household, just to say, "Hey, Dad," or someone to hug you, or to be there with you in those times when you really need him.

Taylor, in "Black Youth Role Models and the Social Construction of Identity" (1989), confirmed the findings of this study that when the father is not a positive role model for a youth, the youth repudiates the father's behavior; therefore, the "father's role as negative role model was often just as influential in shaping the behavior, values and identity aspirations of the youth" (p. 163). By rejecting the father's values and conduct, the youth became highly motivated to take a different direction:

I also had to outlive the shadow of my father, because many people said that I would be just like my dad. But he had his lifestyle and I had mine. [His lifestyle is] one that I am not proud of—I would not allow people to push me into his lifestyle. I hung with my father for a while, I would see the things he was doing. What I saw him do, somehow it stuck deep within me that I didn't have to do those things. I could do the opposite. By hanging out with my dad and learning things that he was doing and watching how he dealt with people, I went in a different direction. . . . So, I would not allow people to plan my life for me. I decided what I wanted to be and who I wanted to be. I set out to accomplish that; thus far it's working to my advantage.

*   *   *

[My father] was dealing drugs, and he said that he didn't have any money, but he can give me something, you know, to turn a profit on [when respondent needed money]. So, that was one of the major things that turned me off from him and turned me into the person I am right now. The father I am right now [respondent has two sons].

In "Coming Up as a Boy in the Ghetto" (1991), David A. Schulz stated that a black youth in the ghetto

strives to assert his masculinity against almost overwhelming handicaps. . . . If he is in his late teens, he has seen in himself what he feared he saw all along in his father—a person ill-prepared to "go it alone." . . . These men, furthermore, are handicapped in teaching their sons a legitimate means of earning a living. . . . [Frequently] no young boy coming up would want "to be what his father was." (pp. 7, 10)

Significant findings of the research reviewed in this section, and the present study as a whole, were the following:

* Someone in school took a personal interest in students' work (mentor teachers).
* The students work hard in school.

- The students see academic achievement as a way out of depressed and dangerous environments.
- Personal importance of athletics.
- Subjects "walk a fine line" in their community; the most threatening aspect of their community life is drug trafficking.
- Students stay by themselves, away from gangs.
- Students do not have peers with whom they are really close; they are relatively isolated.
- When the fathers are in the home, the fathers serve as role models and strongly influence the child.
- If fathers do not live up to a positive role model for a youth, the youth repudiates the father's behavior.
- Someone in the family actively cares.
- Students' family is defined broadly to include extended relations.

In the other studies cited, the need for a father is not discussed; however, in this study, the students who did not have a father in the home expressed a strong "need" for one.

THE LINK TO A CARING MENTOR OR ROLE MODEL

In the present study, the major influences in respondents' lives other than family and church were coaches and teachers:

My twelfth grade teacher . . . [was a] black male teacher. . . . He was always asking me where is my self-esteem, and in that way, that made me think about what was self-esteem, and try to gain it.

* * *

Dr. H . . . [was my] math teacher . . . [in my] sophomore year in high school. . . . He stayed there, . . . he kept me after school. . . . He wanted to make sure that I learned my math—just the integrity that he has. He pushed me to do my best—self-motivation.

* * *

[Teachers] . . . would always tell me, there's a tough world out there. . . . You gotta really work hard, you gotta really listen, you gotta really pay attention to what they're saying, 'cause what somebody's saying is really something you're gonna need in life.

* * *

I really had a tough time in math, and this teacher, he helped me out a lot. He was patient, he was loving, he was kind, and all the things that a teacher should possess.

* * *

I had a very, very good coach, DB. He brought us up to understand life. . . . What we should do is set our sights on life, and get the job done, is how he said it. Get the job done. Don't go around beating around the bush and procrastinating, but go in there, and get the job done, and feel good about yourself. The experience he gave us through basketball, we can relate to life. . . . That's how I see it. He taught me how to be prepared, how to work hard, also a work ethic—he always told me to work hard, work hard at everything.

* * *

Coach J and Coach M, they always give you a pat on the back when you did good; but they wouldn't emphasize it, because they know you could do so much better, so that kept you striving and working hard trying to improve yourself, and the coach out here is the same way, he'll pat you on the back every now and then, but, at the same time, he knows that you can do so much better, so he pushes you and stays on your case.

As H. P. McAdoo (1988) noted about black-families research by Wilhelmina Manns, "Supportive Roles of Significant Others in Black Families," although a vital kinship network "support[s] overall survival and coping efforts" in black families, other individuals, who are not relatives, are committed to the achievement of the young person and are an integral part of their lives. The largest group of non-relative significant others (47 percent) is in the field of education.

Students' answers indicated that teachers and coaches worked with them and instructed them to "work hard, "really listen," and "set our sights on life." When speaking about their coaches, the emphasis is on the word "good": a "very, very good coach." Through the students' words, a relevant theme emerged that both teachers and coaches established a "caring" relationship with the student.

The bond between mother and son, the link to religion, the link to family, and the link to a caring mentor or role model were the fundamental themes that emerged from the data.

ACHIEVEMENT MOTIVATION

Examining Achievement Motivation Theories in Cross-Cultural Research

Castenell (1984), in his article "A Cross-Cultural Look at Achievement Motivation," reviewed literature on the theoretical assumptions about achievement. He cited David McClelland and others, who in 1947 interpreted achievement motivation "as a learned motive, unconscious in nature, resulting from reward or punishment for specific behavior" (p. 436). McClelland found that "achievement motivation is formed in early childhood experiences, and that parents who teach independent mastery, a sense of competition, and reward such behavior are giving their children achievement training" (p. 436). The researchers that McClelland cited concluded that while some youngsters have a need to achieve, others do not.

Castenell also cited Fritz Heider (1958), who departed from conventional assumptions and theorized that the way in which an individual behaves is contingent on the individual's expectation of success or failure. He named four attributes significant in predicting behavior: ability, effort produced, difficulty involved, and simple luck. In studies of race differences, DuCette and Walk (1972) and Williams and Stack (1972) asserted that the "internal/external dimension" within the attributional framework—ability, effort, task difficulty, and luck—is the dimension most often used. Castenell added that within this dimension, "internals are more likely to achieve because they believe that they are in control of their lives, while externals believe that fate is beyond their control" (p. 438). Although numerous studies reported that blacks are more external than whites, the present study revealed that the students took charge of their own lives (internal dimension). In doing so, the students exhibited their ability to make choices and to focus on goal-oriented behavior.

Castenell's major emphasis in analyzing researchers who make comparisons of ethnic groups was that a built-in ethnocentrism exists, which is difficult to overcome, especially when the researcher does not take into account unique aspects of the cultures being studied. For example, in the scoring system of TAT (Murray's Thematic Apperception Test), "values such as delayed gratification are scored as achievement, but values such as cooperation (or collectivity) are not scored as achievement" (p. 437).

Castenell also mentioned the self-report measure (e.g., the Rotter I-E scale, the Bialer scale, and Nowicki-Strickland Locus of Control), which is also used to assess achievement; however, he stated that the self-report measure has many problems: "Too often, the achievement tasks used and the criterion of success are individual tasks on which success is the result of one's own actions and attributes, rather than cooperative or group achievement tasks on which success is the result of joint efforts" (p. 440). Nevertheless, Castenell argued that minority groups such as blacks, females, and the lower class are primarily socialized to value cooperation; therefore, they are less oriented to individualistic behavior than the dominant group. Castenell included other researchers, such as Guttentag and Klein (1976), who concluded that the self-report assessment is commonly standardized on a white, non-urban population, and also Gurin and Epps (1975), who stated that "black students possess collective and individual orientations for achievement, unlike whites" (p. 440). In the present study, the black family exhibited a collective orientation, and the students also professed a collective orientation; nevertheless, they demonstrated the ability to be individualistic, if the need arises. They therefore embraced the values of the majority/white culture, as well as the minority/black culture.

In a section on comparative studies of blacks and whites, Mussen (1953), who investigated the differences between TAT responses, concluded that "blacks perceived the world as hostile and threatening" (p. 437). Blacks males, then, have inner struggles as well as outer obstacles to confront, which dissipates their energies. The present study finds that the theme of survival, or survival skills, is a primary factor in the scheme of success for inner-city black youth. Researchers need to consider the probability that the black male has, in order to achieve, a significantly stronger desire (as well as drive) to succeed than most other groups.

The sample of African-American males in this study literally and figuratively rejected any negative influences, even their peers and fathers, if peers' and fathers' actions would be detrimental to their well-being. The successful student made distinct choices to "go in the opposite direction." In this manner, this sample of black students confirmed their ability to function alone, if necessary. They have a strong sense of Self (internal dimension).

Castenell posited alternative suggestions that would refute ethnocentric assumptions. He believed that goals and causes will be different for different groups and that the catalyst for achieving is unique to different groups. As for controls for ethnocentric assumptions, he said, the first point to take into consideration would be the interaction between the individual and the individual's situational/contextual factor. This would give alternative interpretations for diverse achievement patterns of youngsters. For example, it is possible to score low on a general measure of achievement motivation while at the same time scoring high on a specific context of achievement. Thus, some blacks may score lower than some whites on an academic achievement motivational measure but demonstrate a high level of achievement motivation in sports.

What would be the reasons for a concentration on sports? The students in this study said that they were highly motivated by sports in that they envisioned success in athletics as a way to get out of the inner city. The students also reported that they learned about life through their coaches, who in many cases were their mentors and their male role models. Therefore, in this case, the black males' choices for achievement would be different from those of white males, as the groups are socialized in different environments (situational/contextual factors). Circumstances and situations in which achievement behavior occurs need to be more fully understood.

Castenell further discussed the consensus/conflict factor, asserting that three sociocultural domains—the family, the school, and the peer group—influence youth in their performance. He indicated, however, that different expectations prevail for different ethnic groups. For example, for white middle-class males the selection of a specific area and school success are approved and reinforced by all three socializing agents. Although "many black families expect their children to do well in school, given the families' past experience with the school system, as well as the school's modest expectation of their children's success, a situation is created whereby the children are not likely to channel all their resources into academic success" (p. 441). Consequently, many of these youngsters shift their interests in other directions and become a part of the statistical one in four that do not succeed. A supportive environment is therefore necessary for success.

Castenell's review of the literature showed that reinforcement or consensus is important for the decision-making process, and if the family, the school, and the peer group give "different signals" a conflict will exist for the adolescent. Although the black adolescent may look to all three socializing agencies, the family is the most positive support agency for black youth.

Castenell summarized his research in "A Cross-Cultural Look at Achievement Motivation Research," stating that "the need to achieve is not buried in one's subconscious, but is shaped by social agencies and significant others . . . [and that] the need to achieve is universal to all groups, but because different groups have different life experiences, it is likely that the situations or a set of tasks will evoke different group responses" (p. 442).

He used an investigation of his own to provide evidence that the sociopsychological approach has merit. The sample selected was 310 subjects from the eighth grade in three junior high schools; it provided an adequate distribution of adolescents by race, sex, and socioeconomic status. The measure constructed was a nine-item general achievement motivation scale, composed of three three-item subscales (peer, home, and school) that represented specific areas of possible achievement. Results supported the theory that blacks perceived achievement differently from whites. Specifically, blacks perceived the importance of achieving in all three areas—peer, home, and school—whereas whites perceived the need to achieve only in the area of school (p. 443). Yet, the sample of black male students in this study reflected their need to achieve in education. In this way, "success" was school achievement, the same as in the majority culture.

Different ethnic groups have different catalysts for achievement and therefore different levels of achievement for similar tasks, depending on the individuals' perceptions through their own cultural filters. Instead of relying solely on quantitative measurements to deduce comparisons and contrasts, researchers need to implement a qualitative approach, such as narrative inquiry and a holistic perspective. This study of success factors is a reliable indication that minorities should be heard qualitatively as well as quantitatively.

Coping and Resilience

In an article entitled "Against the Odds: A Profile of Academic Achievers from the Urban Underclass" (1989), Pollard asserted (using data collected by a survey questionnaire of 361 minority students from the urban underclass) that their achievement reflects resilient coping with stress. Pollard noted that the high achievers in her study can be seen as young people "under stress as a result of their poor and castelike minority status." The sample was taken from five middle and five high schools in a large midwestern city. The students chosen were minority, black or Hispanic, with a grade-point average 2.5 or above, and of low enough socioeconomic status to be eligible for free or reduced-price school lunches. She claimed that "these students have managed to achieve academically in spite of the odds stacked against them by society and often by the schools" (p. 307). She cited the works of Werner (1984), *Young Children*, and Garmezy (1985), "Stress-Resistant Children: The Search for Protective Factors," which corroborated her findings that if positive self-perceptions and support from others are in place, a youth, although exposed to an enormous amount of stress, can sustain resilient behavior, and that academic achievement reflected their ability to channel their stress in positive ways. Wilson-Sadberry, Winfield, and Royster (1991), in "Resilience and Persistence of African American Males in Postsecondary Enrollment," reported the factors important for academic success: "parents' general level of encouragement and concern, students' belief in the work ethic, religious convictions[,] . . . belief in themselves, participation in class and in extracurricular activities (particularly athletics), good coping skills, motivation, and determination" (p. 90).

In this study not only the factors outlined by Wilson-Sadberry et al. hold true, but also the factors of coping and resilience (as discussed in the research by Pollard). The students have incorporated within their psyches their mothers' ability to work hard, to cope with stress, and be resilient. An important factor that emerged throughout the interviews is the students' method of coping with stress. Their involvement in organizations and extracurricular activities, such as the Optimist Club and the Best Buddies program in their youth, gave them a sense of positive self-esteem; their involvement in fraternities and The President's Men in their college years gave them the opportunity to "give back" to the community. However, the students' involvement in athletics surfaced as the most relevant activity; it offered catharsis for stress, helped to keep them out of trouble, opened a way to get out of the inner city, and relieved their pain:

Sports gave me an outlet for my pain from my grandma's death. It can really show you how to be a leader and a team player. . . . It pretty much was my second family.

*   *   *

Sports was the way that occupied my time and that turned me away from the streets. . . . Athletics gave me a sense of going to college. I knew [sports] was the only way I was gonna get out of the ghetto. . . . [It was] a way to get out of the ghetto, a way to become someone and just to give back.

*   *   *

I always enjoyed athletics. It was fun; it kept you out of trouble. . . . Athletics is very positive in my life, because it keeps me in shape; it keeps me focused, and, sometimes, you need to relieve some stress, and you just get out there and run, and sweat and play. . . . You feel a lot better.

*   *   *

By me having a love for sports, most of the time when my friends were doing these negative things, I would take it upon myself to go to the court and play some games of basketball, go to the park and play some football. If I wasn't interested in sports, then that could have easily been my hobby so to speak, those negative things. . . . So that kept me on the right track as far as staying out of trouble. . . . It did keep me out of trouble and kept me busy. . . . If it wasn't for athletics, I probably wouldn't be in college today. . . . Good things . . . positive people . . . good things . . . positive people . . . good things happen.

Through athletics the students are "seen as more of a role model in the community. . . . They would look at me like a role model, because I was a good athlete." Also, the students, through athletic training, were taught "responsibility, setting goals, finishing tasks, and, most important, discipline." This training and discipline carried over to other situations in life. It helped to keep the students "on track."

Achievement Motivation from the Students' Perspective

When students were asked the question, "What's inside you that motivates you to succeed?", the themes that emerged from the students' responses were "family," "something better," "something inside":

First of all, my family. Then I would say my school, because, like they say, "Hard work does pay off" [student works in the courthouse] . . . and I talk to some of the judges, they are very motivating. . . . My involvement with the Student Government Association. . . . The community—being able to interact with some of the youngsters. That's very motivating for me. As a matter of fact, that's the number one priority. That's why I continue to do it. That's basically it. My family, you know, it's in my heart; it's in my heart.

* * *

I like to do it myself. I work hard. It's a lot that I expect out of life, and it's a lot I intend to achieve out of life—and, I don't feel like anything can stop me. I think, just more or less self-motivation. It gotta be from within. . . . Well, I really think what really motivated me is that a lot of people in the world today do not expect a black man to really make it. . . . That really motivates me and makes me work hard to achieve my goals.

* * *

Well, when I see my mother and my grandmother . . . they really worked hard to get me the things that I needed out of life, and when I see that, I feel I want to make life for them better. . . . I can't let them down. I have to keep on going and sometimes when I get tired, I think of them—I have to keep going and push myself, so I can be a person to them, so I can take care of them sometimes, so they can relax for all the good work they've done in bringing me up.

The students' thoughts returned to the archetype set by their families of "hard work," the importance of "someone caring," and the significance of proving that they can "make it."

The Cluster I students interviewed (the seventeen students born in the continental United States) exhibited bonding to mother, grandmother, and family in general; they also exhibited determination, coping skills, and resilience. They have made choices to take paths that have led them to an education and a purposeful future.

DISTINGUISHING CHARACTERISTICS BETWEEN CLUSTER I AND CLUSTER II

Although the major emphasis of this study was on African-American males, The President's Men organization also had members born outside the United States. This allowed an opportunity to collect data on the distinguishing characteristics of the two groups, to discover themes common to both, and to establish themes that unite them. Therefore, both the seventeen students born inside the United States (Cluster I) and the seventeen born outside the country (Cluster II) were interviewed. In this section of the study, SAS was used to collate the demographics from the students' biographical forms.

Place of Birth of Cluster I and Cluster II Students

Cluster I consisted of seventeen students born in the United States: Florida (twelve), Alabama (one), Georgia (one), South Carolina (one), Pennsylvania (one), and New York (one). Cluster II consisted of seventeen students born outside of the United States: the Bahamas (seven), Jamaica (four), Tortola in the Virgin Islands (one), St. Thomas in the Virgin Islands (one), Haiti (two), Nicaragua (one), and Scotland (one).

The Age of Cluster I and Cluster II Students

The average age of Cluster I students was 23.8 years; the average for Cluster II students was 24.5 years.

Percentage of Time the Students Had Been Raised by Their Grandparents

In Cluster I, the grandmother was involved in raising the child 56.1 percent of the time; the grandfather was involved 34.2 percent of the time. In Cluster II, the grandmother was involved in raising the child 64.9 percent of the time; the grandfather was involved 47.3 percent of the time. In both clusters the grandmother was more involved in the raising of the student than the grandfather, but the grandfather did serve as a role model, as reflected in the interviews.

Grade-Point Averages for Cluster I and Cluster II Students

The grade-point average of Cluster I and Cluster II students was almost identical. The average for Cluster I was 3.06; the average for Cluster II was 3.16.

The Parental Household Type by Place of Birth

In Cluster I, of the seventeen students, ten (58.82 percent) had been raised in single-parent homes, and seven (41.18 percent) had been raised in two-parent homes; in Cluster II, of the seventeen students, five (29.41 percent) had been raised in single-parent homes, twelve (70.59 percent) in two-parent homes. These percentages are significant in that there was a two-to-one ratio (10:5) of single-parent homes in Cluster I over Cluster II. The statistics developed in this study did not reveal any achievement differences between students from single-parent homes and two-parent homes.

Parents' Educational Level

In Cluster I, of the seventeen mothers, the educational level was as follows: junior high school (two), senior high school (nine), college (four), and graduate school (two). Of the seventeen fathers, the educational level was: elementary school (one), junior high school (one), senior high school (seven), college (three), and graduate school (one); four students did not respond to that question. In Cluster II, of the seventeen mothers, the educational level was: elementary school (one), junior high school (three), senior high school (seven), and college (five); one student did not respond. Of the seventeen fathers, the educational level was: junior high school (two), senior high school (eight), college (four), and graduate school (one); two students did not respond. In Cluster I, 52.94 percent of the mothers had attended senior high school; in Cluster II, 43.75 percent had done so. In Cluster I, 53.85 percent of the fathers had attended senior high school; in Cluster II, 53.33 percent had. The educational levels of the parents in the two clusters were similar.

Family Yearly Income

In Cluster I, of the fourteen families (three students did not respond to the question), the yearly income of two families was less than $10,000 dollars; for four families it was between $10,000 and $20,000; for two families, between $20,000 and $30,000; and the yearly income of six families was between $30,000 and $40,000. In Cluster II, of the seventeen families, the yearly income of five families was less than $10,000; for three families it was between $10,000 and $20,000; for two families, between $20,000 and $30,000; for four families, between $30,000 and $40,000; and the yearly income of three families was $40,000 or more (the amount above $40,000 was not elicited). In family income, between $10,000 and $40,000, the clusters were similar.

Integration versus Segregation in Elementary School

Of the seventeen students in Cluster I, fourteen responded to the question, "Did you attend a segregated elementary school?"; ten reported that their elementary school had been integrated (71.43 percent). In Cluster II, all seventeen students responded to the question; thirteen students indicated that they had attended an integrated elementary school (76.47 percent).

Integration versus Segregation in Junior or Mid-School

Of the seventeen students in Cluster I, in response to the question, "Did you attend a segregated junior or mid-school?" (three students did not respond), eleven indicated that they had attended an integrated junior or mid-school (78.57 percent). In Cluster II, all seventeen students responded to the question; fifteen reported that they attended an integrated junior or mid-school (88.24 percent).

Integration versus Segregation in High School

Of the seventeen students in Cluster I, in response to the question, "Did you attend a segregated high school?" (three students not responding), eleven students responded that they attended an integrated high school (78.57 percent). In Cluster II, all seventeen students responded to the question; they all indicated that they attended an integrated high school (100 percent). Cluster I and Cluster II responses indicated that a majority of the students graduated from an integrated elementary school, an integrated junior or mid-school, and an integrated senior high school; all of these students enrolled in college.

Teachers Contribution to Success

Of the seventeen students in Cluster I, in response to the question, "Did teachers contribute to your success?", twelve (85.71 percent) said Yes. (Three students did not respond to the question.) In Cluster II, all seventeen responded to the question and sixteen (94.12 percent) said Yes.

The SAS report confirmed the interview responses of the students in both clusters in which they stated a need for mentors and role models, which included their teachers and coaches.

Full-Time versus Part-Time Students

In Cluster I, of the seventeen students, sixteen (94.12 percent) were full-time, and one was part-time. In Cluster II, of the seventeen students, sixteen (94.12 percent) were full-time, and one was part-time.

Marital Status

In Cluster I, two students were married (four students did not respond); in Cluster II, one student was married (one student did not respond to the question).

Students' Major Area of Study, Clusters I and II

The students' choices of a major area of study were diverse: they included philosophy, education, criminal justice, accounting, psychology, business administration, computer science, physical education, special education, airway computer science, public administration, mathematics, biology, and data-base management.

Distinct Concepts That Emerged from Interviews of Cluster I and Cluster II

Some emerging concepts in Cluster II differed from emerging concepts in Cluster I; therefore, the distinctions were taken into account.

For Cluster I students, the theme of bonding to a significant individual in their life emerged as of primary importance to their success and survival. The students also asserted that they endeavored to excel in order to overcome the stereotype of black males that they see and hear in the media. Cluster II students expressed a need to excel to meet the expectations of their family and because it was important to "achieve in the eyes of the community."

In Cluster I, seven of the seventeen students' fathers resided in the home, and the students whose fathers did not reside in the home revealed a strong "need" for a father. The fathers who resided in the home were depicted by the students as their role models. In Cluster II, twelve of the seventeen fathers resided in the home. The father's role in the family emerged as being relevant to keeping the student "on track." The students referred to their fathers in such words as the "only breadwinner," enforcing a "lot of discipline," "great role model," "my idol," "very strict," "molded me," "had a very heavy hand"; he is "the main factor"; [he] "had a very strong influence," [he] "made a lot of sacrifices"; "my father played the traditional father role—disciplinarian and breadwinner"; the "enforcer"; the "wrath of my father forbade me," "conditioned [me]"; "I've taken [his] ability to push onward and keep going despite the odds, despite how difficult it is," [I have a] "tremendous fear of being punished, absolutely, very tremendous fear."

In Cluster I, the mother is the archetype of hard work, integrity, determination, perseverance, strength, and character. The mother was also strict in her upbringing of the child so that the son could survive the hostile environment that they were living in. In Cluster II, regarding the respondents' mother, the themes that emerged were mother's guidance, control, and expectations: "mother would sit [the children] around the table and teach them things"; "mother expected me to be an obedient child"; mothers had "high expectations"; father and mother had "ultimate control"; mother is the "inspiration, motivating me, like a best friend, talks to me, keeps me going"; "strict"; "she never let us out of her sight." A sense of "strictness," a rigidity embedded within the society itself, emerged as a significant theme within the context of the interviews.

The following comments from a student revealed the differences between athletics for students in the United States and for students outside the United States:

The athletic scene is not as developed in Jamaica as is the American scene; we don't have the NBA, nor the NFL as it's called; we don't have all those things in Jamaica, and baseball; the most important event that we have is track and field and most of our athletes have done very well in the Olympics over the years.

Here, the Cluster II students' emphasis regarding sports was in track and field and soccer. Football was referred to as "American football."

Coaches were convincing role models for students in Cluster I while the students were growing up; fathers were convincing role models for students in Cluster II while the students were growing up; however, when the Cluster II students entered college and were involved in sports activities, the students "listened" and "learned" from the coaches, like Cluster I students.

Cluster I respondents referred to growing up in government-subsidized housing projects, but the word *project* never appeared in the Cluster II interviews. The term *ghetto* was often referred to by the Cluster II students as the place where they lived (although no segregation exists). Ghetto in this sense referred to "low income" communities, "houses close to each other." A ghetto area was also described as the "inner city ghetto area [where] there were drugs and crime"; "it's not [like] living on the hillside with the sea in the backdrop." One of the respondents said, "I can characterize myself as a ghetto child"; "poverty level, poverty neighborhood."

From studying the term *community* within the context of the students' statements, different concepts emerged. Cluster I students referred to the community not in the context of achieving "in the eyes of the community," but in the sense of "helping" in the community, "giving back" to it. The idea of achieving "in the eyes of the community" emerged in Cluster II responses: "I want to be successful for people in my community; they put pressure on you to be successful"; "I'm from the ghetto, a poor place; they respect you only to see you become doctors and lawyers—to say he's from my community."

In Cluster I, students live in neighborhoods in which violence and drugs are a part of their daily lives, and they are taught how to survive, sons by mothers, how to "make it" through the day. In Cluster II, students live in lower-middle-class "ghetto" neighborhoods; they are not exposed to the random violence experienced by Cluster I students, particularly African-American students living in what is referred to as the "inner city."

In Cluster I, the students used figurative language that implied a desire to escape their environment. In Cluster II, the students' language was not metaphorical.

The following chapter analyzes the African-American students' words metaphorically. The statements from the students are grounded in the obstacles that they had to overcome, and they reveal how the students coped with those obstacles.

5

Analysis, Conclusions, and Recommendations

METAPHORS

Analysis of Metaphors in the Study

Embler (1966) defined metaphors as figurative expressions that give meaning to words; he described the metaphor as a fleeting image with an enduring thought. He explained that words do more work than the utterance itself, in that many expressions have intuitive connotations, and these hidden meanings, if examined, can reveal knowledge about "ourselves and our worlds" (p. 58).

As examples of his ideas, Embler referred to images in literary works which give powerful statements that describe society. An illustration that Embler used is Plato's "cave"; he interpreted the "cave" as a prison metaphor (p. 59).

In this inquiry, the cave as prison metaphor fits; the theme of survival underscores the inquiry as the Cluster I students created images of a confining enclave, which was the world they grew up in. They speak about their exposure to drugs, gangs, violence, and death within their world. (However, throughout their young lives, they surmount these menacing obstacles by focusing their energy on staying safe and steering clear of danger.)

I was in a close knit environment, where I just thought what was going on in the world was right on my block. Everything was just happening on my block. . . . I had a heavy block. There was a gang on one corner. And in the middle of the block, they ran illegal numbers, and at the end of the block, there were drug dealers. This was all on one block.

* * *

There was a lot of things I had to walk through everyday, going to school and coming back home. The gang problem was the one that really took a lot of black kids to jail. Kids that I grew up with—that I don't think I'll ever see again, 'cause they're in jail for very bad things that they did. So, the gang problem was the number one issue. . . . I had no vision of what was outside or what was tomorrow. I just lived for the today.

* * *

Death . . . it was out there. It could happen just like that. . . . [My mother] wanted me to survive and become a great person. She wanted her son. As she tells me, "You're my only son," and she has to keep me. That's mainly why, I think, she kept me away from trouble, mainly death.

* * *

I guess I could have easily turned to the street life, because the life I grew up with, I had to learn the streets at an early age, so I guess the streets could have been one obstacle that could have shot at my success, but I have a strong mind, and I have a will to succeed, so I guess that's one reason I didn't turn to the streets. [In a discussion after the recorded interview, the student spoke about the government projects that he lives in "like a prison." He was born in the projects and still lives there.]

* * *

I did not see a road, a path, or whatever word you would like to use. I didn't see anything. The only thing I saw was that it was more important for me to stay out of trouble, than it was for me to worry about would it be a better day.

* * *

I think right now he's [speaking about a friend] on drugs, but those are some of the major differences in my household than my friend's household. The guy didn't even have a chance, because one of his sisters passed away. She got murdered, and they threw her body somewhere—this was when I was living in the projects—threw her body somewhere in some dumpster by their house.

Embler also discussed expressions that are metaphors of motion; he used examples of words such as "beyond" and "further," which, he said, imply a desire for change (p. 32). This research shows that regardless of the many circumstances that could have conceivably pulled the respondents down, their words connote effort and change: "reach," "push forward," "grasp," "steer."

Dreams. . . . *reach for it.* . . . Take a stand, *go for it.* . . . Put in the time . . . *reach.* . . . *grasp* . . . *push forward.* . . . To stay on the outside . . . not be incarcerated. . . . [Lay] out your yellow brick road. . . . *Reach . . . just touch it, grasp . . . get it.* . . .

* * *

I guess, by me visualizing them . . . [prisoners in Dade County Jail—he is employed at the Dade County Courthouse] . . . and seeing the predicament that they're in, I know I would never want to be there, so that definitely has *to make me push forward*, to make sure I do what I have to do to stay on the outside, and not be incarcerated, or anything of that nature.

* * *

I always envisioned myself going to college and *to really get out* of that kind of environment . . . a negative neighborhood. . . . I saw that [my aunt] worked very hard, and I could tell that she wasn't happy where she was at, and that it wasn't too good of a place. More reason *to inspire me to try* and help myself *to move out* of that neighborhood.

* * *

Most of the things you can sense—you see things that happen on the street, like little arguments that you see might turn out to something, you must *move away* from, or, because most of the people I knew, they carried guns and did bad things.

* * *

I saw a lot. I learned *to weed my way* away from the wrong crowd simply by sitting back and observing what's going on. You can sit back and observe and tell something's not right.

Lakoff and Johnson (1980) discussed "orientational metaphors," which have a "spatial orientation"—for example, "up-down," "in-out." They used illustrations such as "health and life are up," and "sickness and death are down" (p. 14). The responses that the students gave to interview questions also reflected the use of "spatial metaphors." These metaphors described the respondents' circumstances: "up" is uplifting; "down" is negative, or death; "in" is safe; "out" is unsafe.

Mom, I'm just feeling bad [down] about this, and she would talk to me, . . . she would *lift* me *up*.

* * *

[The] stereotypical attitude that society has against African-American males . . . every day, you have a lot of African-American males, like myself, that are *striving* [up] to be successful and be a positive role model and have an objective in life. . . . You have other that are *tearing* us *down*.

* * *

Being *out* [in the streets] there would take me away from my *vision* of my future. . . . My mother always required that I be *in* the house before dark.

* * *

So, mostly when I tend to see something flare up, [I] just go *inside*. I overcame [the neighborhood]. I just—I looked *above* [up] that. I looked at it as being somebody in life and not worrying about anybody *below* [down] me.

* * *

It's amazing what you can do when you *elevate* your mind. When you *elevate* yourself *above* that what you're in. *Elevation* is beautiful, because it's *Progressive*; you keep going like a ladder *higher* and *higher*—people don't understand that, but I would tell them *to go for the gusto*.

In explaining these expressions as metaphors, the implication is that the use of the words "up-down" and "in-out" symbolized the internal struggle, and perhaps subconscious desire, to cope with and survive difficult obstacles. Embler stated that many individuals are inclined to perceive life "as a struggle for existence, to be *HIGH UP* is to be *ABOVE*, literally, the struggle" (p. 30) and that the use of metaphorical terms discloses hidden desires and goals.

Lakoff and Turner (1989) discussed two common metaphors: *Purposes Are Destinations* and *Life Is a Journey*. Regarding *Purposes Are Destinations*, they stated that "A purposeful life has goals, and one searches for means toward those goals." They conceived "of the means to those destinations as paths" (p. 3). They mentioned common expressions, "doing things in a roundabout way" and "working our way around obstacles" (p.3), as goal-oriented. In the same vein, they spoke of the metaphor *Life Is a Journey*, explaining that it not only incorporates the idea that "purposes are destinations" in the journey but also the thought that the "choices in life are crossroads" (p. 4).

The themes that emerged in this study which correspond to the above metaphors are the students' attitude toward a "purposeful life," "goal-oriented behavior," and "meaningful choices":

[I] started studying people. If what they did would get them into trouble, *I would watch it*, and *I would do the opposite. . . . I used the life that people lived . . . to try to straighten out my life.*

* * *

First thing, to overcome an obstacle, is just like making a decision. Decision-making. First, you have to define the obstacle, analyze the obstacle, and then you have *to establish alternatives to overcome the obstacle*, and whichever alternatives suits you best, *that's the way to go.*

* * *

I guess that would depend on the obstacle, but *I think I would just sit back* and *just think about it*, and *just analyze the situation*, and weigh my advantages and disadvantages, and *I think I'd come up with the right decision.*

Illustrations of the "paths" that the respondents chose surfaced in their decision-making regarding peers, many of whom "went the wrong way." They observed peers' behavior and made choices not to follow them.

My peers . . . a lot of them are dead. . . . I find that a lot of them are in jail—quite a few on the streets hooked on drugs or selling drugs. . . . *I look at that* and I say *they didn't succeed*, so, if I could succeed, hopefully, it would give them [others] some incentive to achieve.

* * *

I had peer pressure, as far as dealing with drugs. I had people come to me, "Will you like to smoke a drug or deal a drug?" . . . Just a matter of saying, *no*, and *just thinking of the consequences* of getting involved in it.

* * *

A few of my friends went the wrong way, but it's not that they was originally bad, they just, more or less, wanted to be bad, wanted to have guns. . . . *I kinda steered away from that.* I didn't have a lot of friends. . . . I spent most of my time in the fields *just running* with my dog. I didn't have a lot, lot of friends.

* * *

I have about seven friends that are in jail. I have about one that has a life sentence. I have several others that are probably going to be in jail for the rest of their lives. . . . *I saw enough of the other side to realize that something else has to be better.* . . . So my friends, yes, they helped me, but in doing negative things, helped me to realize *that that's not the way to go.*

* * *

The negative things that went on in my neighborhood. There were a lot of drug dealings going on. Some of my friends did drugs . . . guys in class doing drugs . . . wrong track. . . . *I stayed on my track.* And *they stayed on their track. . . . I chose the route that I chose.*

Illustrations of the directions that respondents chose also surfaced in regard to their fathers. If their fathers lived troubled lives and were not positive role models, the students "went in a different direction":

I had to outlive the shadow of my father. . . . *He had his lifestyle, and I had mine. . . . It stuck deep within me. . . . I could do the opposite. . . . I went in a different direction.*

* * *

A bad man . . . in and out of jail . . . [my father] was dealing drugs, and he said that he didn't have any money, but he can give me something, you know, to turn a profit on [when respondent needed money]. So that was one of the major things *that turned me off from him* and *turned me into the person I am right now*—the father I am right now.

In the last chapter, "Choices," of his introspective book, *Makes Me Wanna Holler*, Nathan McCall illustrated the fate of neighborhood friends: "Of the ten families living on my street when I was growing up that had young males in their household, four—including my own—have had one or more of those young men serve time" (p. 401). Trying to understand why so many of his peers had gone to jail, he added: "A psychologist friend once explained that our fates are linked partly to how we perceive our choices in life" (p. 402). McCall's words echo the experiences of the students in this study.

MAJOR THEMES

Summary of Major Themes That Cluster I and Cluster II Students Had in Common

The most significant themes that the two groups had in common were: family as the most relevant factor in the students' lives; religion as an important support system and bond; the existence within them of a burning desire to achieve, an inner feeling (intangible); their selection of choices which are goal oriented, for example, education; evidence of their determination, hard work, coping skills, and resilience; a strong desire among them to serve as role models in the community; and a desire to "give back" and inspire younger black males to achieve.

Summary of Major Themes That Emerged from African-American Students

The theme of *bonding* to a mother or grandmother, or both, and a strong belief in religious faith, emerged as a significant factor in regard to the respondent being "successful" to this point in his life.

The theme of someone *caring* is a relevant factor within the lives of the respondents; when a significant person (primarily an older brother or sister, coach, or teacher) showed a "caring" attitude, students listened and learned about how they should conduct themselves in order to survive their obstacles. In many cases, these individuals became the students' role model. If the father was in the home, then the father was named as a role model. Within the realm of "caring," a significant support system emerged, such as mothers, grandmothers, grandfathers, aunts, uncles, and cousins. In this study, the theme of "caring" comes full circle. Even before the students had graduated from college, they expressed a strong interest in "giving back." The students stated that they joined organizations in school, as well as in the community, in order to "give back," to become involved with helping young black males in the community to find their way to an education.

The theme of *choices* is seen throughout the study in the students' choice to take constructive paths. In the section on metaphors, one can see in the students' remarks language that reflected positive choices: "I learned *to weed my way* from the wrong crowd simply by sitting back and observing what's going on"; "some of my friends did drugs . . . [for me, that was the wrong track], *I stayed on my track*. And they stayed on their track. . . . *I chose the route that I chose*."

The theme of *survival* undergirds the study. The theme of surviving the obstacles in the respondents' path is reflected in the mothers' steadfast concern and admonition to the child to "stay inside" or to get involved with positive activities; the son also learned "resilience" and "coping skills" in the home through the examples set by the mother or grandmother, or both.

Although these four themes, *bonding, caring, choices*, and *survival skills* emerged as the relevant themes, the overriding concept of *nurturing* the child is at the nucleus of the study. The gestalt resembles Figure 5.1.

CONCLUSIONS

The following conclusions have been demonstrated to be necessary factors for an African-American male to succeed:

"Nurturing" is at the center of the young black male's ability to survive and overcome his obstacles, many of which are a part of his daily environment. When a young black male is nurtured by a significant person in his life, that creates in him the capability to persist.

The adolescent's "bonding" to the particular person who provides strong guidance and is a positive role model gives the young man a sense of responsibility not to let that person down. It may be mother or grandmother, a family member, a caring mentor, or a role model.

The nurturing individual and his spiritual upbringing give the individual the positive direction that he needs to "stay on track" and to succeed.

The students in this study are introspective; they take charge of their lives, make constructive choices, and focus on goal-oriented behavior.

A supportive environment—the family, the church, and the school—is necessary for success. This study showed that someone has to "care."

Figure 5.1
Nurturing Matrix

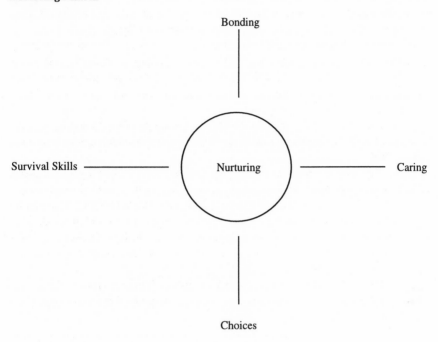

RECOMMENDATIONS

Recommendations of Cluster I and Cluster II Students to Young Black Males in the Community

When students were asked about the recommendations that they had for young black males in the community, the themes that emerged were "be aware of your choices," "stay on the right track," "push hard," "set goals," "stay in school," "be true to yourself," "respect yourself," "follow your dreams," "get off the streets," "hardwork," "determination," "dedication," "get into the books," "you cannot by-pass education," "go to school," "speak to individuals," and "seek out role models."

Recommendations Garnered from the Research

As indicated in this study, the factor of role modeling and mentorship is meaningful in that many black youths do not have a father living in the home. Because of the lack of male role models, black male adolescents are "in search of identity" and "seek someone to follow." The literature also showed that black male youths become disillusioned in school at an early age; they feel that their teachers are indifferent to their achievement and that their teachers should have higher expectations of them. The young black male needs someone who shows concern about him and who has high expectations of him for an extended period of time. Moreover, racism is a factor that he confronts in growing up.

Another important implication of this study on success factors of African-American students reinforced Taylor's (1989) view that many teenagers do not have confidence and trust in others who are in their social environment. Nevertheless, the majority of students in this study have individually expressed that they wished to "give back."

As a follow-up of the considerations discussed and the themes that emerged in this study, the following are recommended to foster the black male students' success in education:

It is vital that teachers have a strong commitment to helping the students achieve.The black male student needs a nurturing environment throughout his school experience. Teachers on all levels have to bond with the student. They should demonstrate concern about him and have high academic expectations of him. Teachers should also discuss any frustrations that may be hindering the student's educational development and help him develop his pride and identity as an individual.

Teachers should learn about the student's culture, implement cultural readings into the curriculum, and communicate to each student in the class that he is important in the teacher's life.

Teachers should "listen" to the student (his verbal and nonverbal behavior), think about what the student is communicating, and believe that the student's words and actions are relevant to his life and his learning.

Cooperative college and public school programs need to be developed in which successful black male college students would go into the public schools and serve as peer role models and peer mentors for young black males. These programs should be instituted and implemented throughout the black male's school experience, beginning when he enters school (first grade). When a young man is stimulated by a competent peer mentor, he has a better chance of reaching his potential.

Historically black colleges, through their fraternities, associations, student governments, and counseling departments, should survey the student body for individuals who want to become involved in existing community projects such as Head Start, JESCA, and TACOLCY to fill the need for male role models.

Honorary organizations such as Florida Memorial College's "The President's Men" should continue to address public school students about the importance of an education and give the young student hope, insight, inspiration, guidance, and also preparation techniques on how to gain entrance into college.

Historically black colleges and black churches need to develop programs where successful black male college students and young black males can interact in the environment of the church. The black church is a natural environment for the young student to communicate his needs.

Basic skills courses—reading, writing, and mathematics—should be a component of every program.

Faculty, administrators, and coaches at historically black colleges should get involved with community mentoring programs such as Miami's 500 Black Male Role Models and 100 Black Men, and they should also encourage their students to participate. In this way, a seed can be planted in the young person's mind that he should consider entering college.

Throughout this study, the process of narrative inquiry revealed stories with similar themes. These similar themes support the concept that a majority of youths raised in a depressed environment have similar experiences. Therefore, there exists between the black male college student and black male adolescent a common ground for positive communication.

Finally, at a time when American society is desperately seeking to alleviate the plight of inner-city black youth, to save a truly lost generation and transform destructive into constructive behavior, this study may serve as an encouragement and a tool for those responsible for teaching and socializing young African-American males who feel that they have little or no chance for success. As there is a critical need for successful black males to serve as positive images, black college students, who have successfully overcome many obstacles in their life to make it to that level of achievement, could help provide the community with needed uplifting role models. Their thoughts on "giving back" to both their own and the larger community can be summed up in one student's remarks:

I want to make a contribution to America, to the community that I live in, to those kids that are less fortunate than I am. . . . I'll be a role model to some little kid who's about to take his life, and I'll end up talking to him and turning his life around. . . . AIDS patients who are dying—if I can go and hold their hand in the last moments of their life so that they can know they don't have to die alone, but that they die with a friend—all these efforts to help humanity would make my life worthwhile. If I could just *steer somebody in the right direction*, then I would know my living is not in vain . . . as long as I can do something for my community, for the people who love me, and for my God.

EPILOGUE

To bring the project to its current (May 1997) status from the initial interviewing sessions, which had taken place from October 1993 to March 1994, I again interviewed Roscoe Warren, director of The President's Men Program at Florida Memorial College. He discussed the continued success of the program and told me that the present members continue to have weekly meetings to discuss relevant issues, such as academic difficulties and social problems. Mr. Warren continues to serve as their mentor and guide, and he attends all their meetings, sometimes as a participant, sometimes as a "listener." He has an open-door policy, and the young men communicate with him all the time. From observation and feedback from the students, it is apparent that he is a special person in their lives. At the college, Mr.

Warren is the Director of Enrollment Management. He is also a respected member of the South Florida community; as noted he is the vice-mayor of Homestead, Florida. He conceived of The President's Men Program for "at-risk" students; the program is one of the components of the Compact Program, which is funded by the Kellogg Foundation and Florida Memorial College. Ninety percent of the students in The President's Men graduate from Florida Memorial College.

The young men in the program continue to reach out in the community. This academic year, 1996–1997, they have adopted Drew Elementary School, where they serve as role models and mentors to the young. They continue to volunteer within the college community as ushers for special events, serve as tutors on the campus, and clean college vehicles to raise money for special projects.

As a follow-up on the current activities of the members of the group that I interviewed in 1994 and 1995, I had recent telephone conversations with the men who had contributed to the initial research. They again responded with candor to my request for data on their personal and professional lives. I requested that they fill out update sheets, which they returned to me. I located all but one student out of the seventeen students in the African-American group, Cluster I; the sixteen students replied. The following biographical information is excerpted from the update sheets, and entries are numbered in order to differentiate among them.

Cluster I Students

1. Attended Columbia Theological Seminary and graduated in May 1997 with a master's of divinity degree; plans to pursue a doctoral degree in the ministry; married, three children; future goal, "pastor with a full-time ministry that seeks to empower African Americans";

2. Counselor for the Metro-Dade County, Florida, Homeless Program; attends Florida International University to obtain a master's degree in criminal justice; married, two children;

3. Attends Federal Law Enforcement Training Center; upon graduation will work as a special agent with the Internal Revenue Service;

4. Social worker; future goal, to pursue a master's degree in public administration;

5. Teaches business education and leadership skills development at Miami Lakes Senior High School, Dade County, Florida, and has been assistant boys' varsity basketball coach for the past three years; future goal, "to get married, have children, become a great husband and father; to pursue a master's degree in educational leadership and obtain an administrative position with the school system";

6. Obtained first accounting job for Carnival Cruise Line in April 1995 (shoreside); September 1996, started new job as a Dade County schoolteacher at Hialeah High School; enrolled at Nova Southeastern University, MBA program; still volunteers as assistant to the athletic coach at Florida Memorial College; also a junior varsity basketball head coach; Pat Riley's book, *The Winner Within*, made him realize that it is okay to dream, but if you do not write down your dreams, they will never become reality—"I had to write down my ambitions, and strive for them; writing down my goals made me realize just how much time I wasted talking about them"; future goal, "I strive to be a major college athletic director; it's written down";

7. Sales representative, warehouse manager, financial consultant; future goal, MBA program and law school;

8. Correctional probation officer, attends Florida International University, pursuing master's degree in criminal justice;

9. Works two jobs, Entenmann's bakery at night and substitute teaching in Dade County; has taken additional courses at Florida International University, in strategic management, production operation management; rejoined church; future goal, pursuing a career in teaching;

10. Systems analyst, Miami-Dade County, Florida;

11. Coaches and teaches at Lee Middle School, Fort Myers, Florida;

12. Graduated from Florida Memorial College, May 1997; NAIA Academic All-American; team captain of FMC varsity basketball team; president of Alpha Kappa Mu National Honor Society; chairman of FMC President's Men; membership director, Accounting Club; Walt Disney/Bryant Gumbel/UNCF scholarship; will attend Southern University's mental health counseling master's degree program, January 1998; since January 1997, substitute teaching;

13. Certified in teaching K–12th grade; currently substitute teaching, working with exceptional children and the learning disabled;

14. Attends Florida Memorial College (senior); two children (unmarried); member of the Dade County Referee Wrestling Association, head coach for the Homestead Park and Recreation Center, bringing wrestling to inner-city children; difficulties, "maintaining full-time status as a college student, without working—no money—the whole family 'depends' on me to graduate and open doors for the next generation of the D family; sometimes the phobia of failing scares me more than surviving"; future goal, "to teach my people the importance of an education; to teach physical education in a Dade County school, open up more black-owned businesses, and open up more job opportunities for minorities";

15. Counseling for one and a half years; now working in a temporary agency to obtain experience in accounting;

16. Teaches computer education for the last eight months at McNicol Middle School, Broward County, Florida; he is also the head basketball coach at the school and enjoyed his first winning season as the head coach; he also began working, successfully, in the telecommunications industry, in which he plans to work full-time within the next five years. He remarks that "Florida Memorial College has given me a jumpstart on my life. I am truly grateful for everything I was able to absorb at FMC. Those years have shaped my views and allowed me to become the person I am today. . . . I will always be involved in coaching in one way or another; I have a tremendous amount of ideas to share with our young people of today."

Cluster II Students

The Cluster II respondents—those born outside the United States—are undertaking diverse occupations: one of them is attending medical school, another one is attending chiropractic school; amongst the group are teachers, an air-traffic controller, an entrepreneur, an accountant, a budget and cost analyst at American Airlines, a computer support technician and trainer, who also automates businesses, and an aide in the Miami-Dade County Manager's Office.

All of the President's Men are continuing their active, busy lives. They are as dynamic now as when they were in college working to obtain their bachelor's degrees. They make every minute in their day count: they work long hours, they express satisfaction in their work, and they look forward to the future with serious and committed goals. Those who have children feel a special responsibility to take care of them and are actively involved in their care. Many of the men are continuing college on a graduate level. All these men are firmly on the path to achievement and success.

Appendix A

Biographical Profile Form

Last Name   First   Middle

Birthdate: Month _____ Day _____ Year_____
Place of birth: United States _____ City _____ State _____

Bahamas _____ Virgin Islands _____
              St. Thomas _____
              St. Croix _____

      Jamaica _____ Haiti _____

      Other _____

If not the United States, what year did you come here?____
The reason for your coming?_____
Major Field of Study: _____
Have you changed your major field of study since entering college? (Yes) _____ (No) _____
If yes, what was your reason for changing? _____

_____

_____

Academic Standing: Freshman _____ Sophomore _____

Junior _____ Senior _____

First semester _____

Second semester _____

How many semesters have you attended college (including this semester)? _____

Grade Point Average: _____

How would you describe your relationship with your teachers at this college? _____

_____

Have your teachers contributed to your success in college? Yes _____ No _____ If yes, in what way _____

_____

_____

Attendance: Full-time _____ Part-time _____

Educational goals: _____

Career goals: _____

Extra-Curricular Activities: Fraternity _____

Community Organization(s) _____

School Organizations(s) _____

Other_____

Of the years that you have been attending college, how many semesters have you been employed?_____

If employed, what have been your occupations?

_____

Student's yearly individual income (from all sources):

_____None _____$1,000–$1,999 _____$2,000–$2,999

_____$3,000–$3,999 _____$4,000–$5,999 _____$6,000–$7,999

_____$8,000–$9,999 _____$10,000–$14,999 _____$15,000 or over

Two-parent home, when growing up: Yes _____ No _____

Single-parent home, when growing up: Yes _____ No _____
If yes,
mother: Yes _____ (or) father: Yes _____

Grandparents were involved in upbringing:
Grandmother: Yes _____ % of time _____ No _____

Grandfather: Yes _____ % of time _____ No _____

Siblings (including self), please state the number: _____ Boys? _____ Girls?_____
Of that number, what number were you? _____
Are you presently married? _____ Do you have any children?_____
If yes, how many? _____

Were the schools that you attended while growing up, segregated (seg) or integrated (integ)?

elementary school (seg) _____ (integ) _____
junior or middle school (seg) _____ (integ) _____
high school (seg)_____ (integ) _____
other_____(seg)_____ (integ)_____

Why did you choose to attend a historically black college?

_____

_____

_____

Parents' educational level:
Mother: Father:
Elementary School _____   Elementary School _____
Junior High School _____   Junior High School _____
Senior High School _____   Senior High School _____
College _____   College _____
Graduate School _____   Graduate School _____

Approximate family yearly income (in American dollars) when you were attending pub-
lic/private school during your high school years:

_____ Under $10,000   _____ $10,000–$14,999

_____ $15,000–$19,999 _____ $20,000–$24,999

_____ $25,000–$29,999 _____ $30,000–$34,999

_____ $35,000–$39,999 _____ $40,000 or over

Religion:_____

Church attendance: _____   _____   _____
                    4x a month   3x a month   2x a month

_____   _____
1x a month   Other

In descending order, please identify the most significant influences (persons, institutions, or other influences) in your life, to date (#1 being the most significant):

1._____   2._____   3._____

4._____   5._____   6._____

Your local telephone number:_____
If residing in the dormitory, please state the name of the
dormitory _____

NOTE: ALL DATA WILL BE HELD IN STRICT CONFIDENTIALITY.

In the research, code numbers, instead of student names, will be used to ensure anonymity.

Code No._____

Appendix B

Selected Interview Transcripts

INTERVIEW 6

Q: What factors contribute to your leadership role and success?

A: Well, I really couldn't say. I think it's just an urge—my urge just to do well. A lot of times when I think I want to give up, I just think back to all the hard times my mom had, certain times when we couldn't pay the rent or something like that. I just think—I just want to do well. There's really not any single factor. I just have that burning desire to do well.

Q: Where did you grow up?

A: As far as when I grew up—well, I grew up in the Liberty City area, and it was hard.

Q: How many years ago are you referring to?

A: I grew up in the early eighties and late seventies, and it was hard on me, because in my neighborhood, there were a lot of gangs. Everybody was getting into gangs, and because my brother did not get into gangs, and my sister always told my brother never to get involved with guys in gangs, I never got involved with them, either. So, I just followed the path. My brother didn't do it, so I didn't do it.

Q: Was that the greatest obstacle you had to overcome, not getting into gangs?

A: Well, that's one, but there were a lot of things going on—like on my block—I had a heavy block. There was a gang on one corner. And in the middle of the block, they ran illegal numbers, and at the end of the block, there were drug dealers. This was all on one block. So there was a lot of things I had to walk through every day, going to school and coming back home. The gang problem was the one that really took a lot of black kids to jail. Kids that I grew up with—that I don't think I'll ever see again, 'cause they're in jail for very bad things that they did. So, the gang problem was the number one issue.

Q: Why did young people join gangs?

A: I really never did know, because I never really did venture into it, but, basically, it was like, you're from this community, you join this gang—you're from another community, you join another gang. Like once they had this big rumble; they called it with the gang that was on my block. They called themselves the Y.O.L—I never knew what the acronym stood for. And there was another gang—it was a Puerto Rican gang. They called themselves the Killer Stones. So, they had a rumble, and I really don't even know. . . . But if you stayed in one neighborhood, you joined this gang; if you stayed in another neighborhood, you joined that gang, and you all just stayed together, 'cause you all grew up together.

Q: And you completely stayed out of gangs?

A: I completely stayed out of gangs. I didn't get involved with gangs at all.

Q: How did you avoid it? Did you have peer pressure to get involved with gangs?

A: Oh, definitely. I had peer pressure trying to get me into gangs, because on my block, I was like more of an athlete, and in small communities, most people, they look up to athletes. Athletes are seen as more of a role model in the community. And, if you're the top athlete, then everybody is looking at you—when there's something going on, they come to you and tell you first. Everything that's going on, they tell to the athletes. Things like in the business world—nowadays, when you're growing up, now you're trying to look for successful men in banking, or whatever, that have made it—not doing something illegal. But when you're young, you don't have those kinds of things, because you're not successful; you just still live under your parents and everything, so when I was around twelve, and someone around six, they would look at me like a role model, because I was a good athlete.

Q: What sports were you good at?

A: Well, football. When I grew up, I grew up definitely into football. There's nothing that could take me away from football. I was a football fan down hard, and later on I switched to basketball, which I'm involved in now.

Q: What schools did you attend while growing up?

A: When I was smaller I went to Shadow Lawn Elementary—that's in Liberty City, then I went to Edison Middle, then I went to Edison Senior High. So, all those are still in the same community. I grew up with the same people.

Q: Were the schools segregated when you were growing up?

A: I wouldn't say that.

Q: Was there a mix?

A: No. There was some, but not enough to really be seen. Shadow Lawn was totally black, Edison Middle was totally black, and my high school was considered black.

Q: Were you getting good grades in public school?

A: Yes. I think it was because of my family structure. My sister was more or less a C student, a C+ student. My brother was more just like a B, and I just saw myself as always—I had to do a little better. So, I was more or less an A/B+ student.

Q: Along with participation in sports?

A: And, sports—my sister was a great athlete in sports. My brother—he really didn't go the sports route. I went the sports route 'cause I used to "hankle" my sister a lot.

Q: Who was your role model? Did you have role models in sports?

A: Tony Dorsett was mine. He's a football player. He played for the Dallas Cowboys. I worshipped Tony Dorsett, because I loved football, but as I grew older, things changed. Now it's Kevin Johnson—Phoenix.

Q: Was your home a two-parent home?

A: No, it wasn't. My father left home when I was real young. I think I remember when he left. I think I was six years old—five or six years old. He left, and it was over from there. So it was just my mom. My mom and us three.

Q: How did your mom manage to take care of the three of you?

A: Oh, she worked hard. She worked two—no, three jobs for like five years, then she cut it down to two. As we got older, she cut it down. Now she only works one, because she doesn't have to work as hard, anymore.

Q: Do you consider her a successful woman?

A: Yeah, she was a hard-working woman.

Q: When you were a little boy could you see outside of your environment? Could you envision what you wanted to be?

A: No. I had no vision of that. I was in a close-knit environment, where I just thought what was going on in the world was right on my block. Everything was just happening on my block. There was nothing—I had no vision of what was outside or what was tomorrow. I just lived for the today.

Q: Did you always know that you were making the right choices, not getting involved in anything negative?

A: Well, back then, I didn't see it—I didn't know what was really good or what was really bad. It was just—I just listened to what my mom said. My mom was like, "Listen, you're going to do this this way and you're not going to ask all these questions—why or why not, 'cause I don't have the answers for you. You just do this this way, and I guarantee you you're going to be all right." So when my brother told me something, or my sister told me something, because they're older than I, I just took that for being the truth.

Q: On your biographical form, you said your father also contributed to your upbringing. How did he contribute?

A: Well, it's because he came around. It was like he always came around at the right time. When it seemed like I was down and out and tired, he always came around and was like, "Listen, I'm gonna have to show you—come with me for a little while." He would take me for three or four days and talk to me, and he would just give me basically man-to-man talks on how life is, and that's how I got my perception on life. When he would take me out of the community, and take me to a different community, and I would just sit down and just realize things.

Q: Did he play an important role, then?

A: Yeah, he definitely played a role.

Q: What kinds of actions did you take to overcome the obstacles when you felt you were being pulled down?

A: Well, a lot of times, my mom, I was able to go talk to my mom, 'cause my mom was willing to listen, so whenever I felt real bad, and my dad wasn't around, I was able to just go in my room and say, "Mom, I'm just feeling bad about this and feeling bad about this," and she would talk to me, and just let me know the options I had to take for that. That's what I would do, and she would lift me up.

Q: Did you win any awards for sports in your public school years?

A: Not major awards, not really. In school, I, basically,—it was math. I had a lot of awards in math and art, too. 'Cause when I was in fourth grade, I was sent to art school, but because I didn't know any students, and I was shy, and I didn't think it was going to work out, I just stopped going. Even though I love to draw. Love to draw. I just drew back from that. In high school, I didn't have any major awards, because I was involved in athletics, but I was never like a star player. I was always the, "Oh, there's B. He plays on the team."

Q: In college, have you won any major awards?

A: Well, not as far as major awards. As far as—two years ago we went to the District as a team, but not as an individual, I haven't won any major awards, individually. But I meant awards, as far as the team structure elected me this, or my team said I was this. I received the MVP [most valuable player] award for the team, for the year, 1993. And I received a leadership award for this year. And I think I would have got an offense award, too, but a friend of mine had one better game than I did. So he edged me out.

Q: What do you see in yourself that led the college to give you a leadership award? How do you see yourself as a leader? Can you look into yourself and say, "These are the qualities I have that make me a leader"?

A: That's hard. Leadership as far as in the community or in the community of the college?

Q: In the college community or just within yourself, generally speaking. What are the qualities you see in yourself?

A: I'm dedicated to everything. If I said to myself, "This is what I'm gonna do, then that's what I'm gonna do." And I'm going to achieve that. I have a way of just going after things. Once I set my mind to it, I'm just going to go after it. And, then, if I don't set my mind to it, then I'm not going to have it. As far as leadership, I believe I can get a leadership award at this college, because dedication, that's one; because I'm very persistent, and that's two; and I have a knack of getting to know people; I can communicate with a lot of people. And once I communicate with people, I can get a leadership award.

Q: What is your grade-point average?

A: My grade-point average is a 3.3.

Q: Are you thinking about graduate schools, presently?

A: Oh, definitely, yes. I've been thinking about graduate school for the last couple of months. I've narrowed my choices down to FAMU [Florida A&M University]. I want to go to FAMU—that's if I don't receive a job, because currently, I'm trying to get into the Dade County School System, and I want to go back to my community, and work there, at Edison, so if that doesn't fall through, then, I think there's a possibility I'll go to FAMU.

Q: If you were offered a corporate position, and a position in the school system simultaneously, which position would you take?

A: I want a position where I could have a chance to work with the kids. I wouldn't want to be in an office. I don't think I want to be in the office. I really want a chance so I can talk to the kids and give them my experiences throughout my life. So I can talk to them and tell them, "This is right, this is wrong, this is the way it should be," and I want to give reasons why this is the way it should be. 'Cause my mom, she told me; she told me different things—to go this way and to go that way—but she never did give me a reason, though I found out the reasons later. I want to be there, so I can tell them this is the reason, and this is the reason, why you should do this. I came from the same environment—I should know.

Q: In speaking to young black males today, or when you get back into your community, what kind of recommendations or messages would you give to them?

A: I would tell them there's a lot of roads to go, and sometimes you want to stay with your friends, and sometimes you have to leave your friends, and I would say, don't think because you leave your friends, that you're doing wrong. Sometimes, in order to get better, there's a possibility that you're gonna leave your friends. But don't forget about them. So, if you make it in the world, always come back and check your friends out, and just stuff like that. Be true to your friends.

Q: What organizations are important to you?

A: Right now I'm part of Kappa . . . fraternity, and I really enjoy being in with them; I enjoy doing the community service that we do around the area, as far as the Best Buddies Program; I enjoy doing that. I enjoy doing this little seminar we had out on campus—the "Don't Drive Drunk" and "Students Against Drunk Drivers." I enjoy doing that. There's just a bunch of volunteer work. I enjoy doing volunteer work where I can help someone, with the knowledge I have as far as—I don't know much, but what I do know, I, at least, try to give it out to other students, so they won't go the wrong way.

Q: Has the church played an important role in your life?

A: Well, as I was growing up, I was very church-oriented, but because of a lot of things I've gotten into, playing basketball, trying to keep my books up, then working, I never really had time to go to church on a regular basis, but I do go to church once or twice a month, at least.

Q: Who are your role models, other than the football players you mentioned?

A: As far as in sports. When I think of sports, they are those, but as far as when I think of education, or not as in education, but as in the business world, I don't have any single role model. It's like—I look at—wherever I go—like right now I'm at Citibank, and one of my role models there is a woman by the name of Paulette. Paulette Hicks. And you know, I look at her, and I see she's a black lady, and she's making it at a Citibank; she's working hard, and I just look at that, and that inspires me to work harder to be equal to, or even better than her. As far as the way she carries herself, the way she presents herself, her attitude, it just remains constant. She's never real mad one day, or she's never real sad one day; she tries to keep her attitude in a nice friendly manner every day. And then if I go to another—someone else—and I come upon a person who fits that role model position, then I just take them on as a role model.

OBSERVER'S COMMENTS

Student was dressed informally; he wore a white t-shirt, with words, "Man on the go" and "Club hopping" initialed on it; he had purchased the t-shirt in Nassau while on vacation; he wore cotton denim jeans, red and black Miami Heat NBA basketball cap, jogging shoes and a gold necklace.

Although his father had left the home when the respondent was a young child, the respondent's father played an important role in his life, being with him at many right times to give him insight into life.

The respondent could not "see" outside his immediate environment. He felt the neighborhood was the "universe."

The respondent was a caring person in that he wanted to "give back" to neighborhood youth when he was ready for a career.

INTERVIEW 22

Q: Where were you born?

A: Miami, Florida.

Q: In what neighborhood?

A: Well, I was born in Overtown, lower-income population. I never really grew up in the neighborhood. I was just born there—in the neighborhood.

Q: Where did you grow up?

A: My younger years, I stayed in an—not an orphan home, but I stayed in a home; I was raised by foster parents until the age of six, and I moved around to about three different foster homes. At six years old, I was taken by my aunt, and from then on, I stayed in Liberty City in the projects.

Q: Do you know why you were placed in the foster home?

A: Well, I was told, but the story never came clear.

Q: Have you met your mother and father?

A: Yes. I met them both.

Q: Did your mother take any role in your upbringing?

A: My mother. No, not really. But, I still have a relationship with her.

Q: Did your father play any role in your upbringing?

A: None.

Q: None?

A: None at all.

Q: Can you describe the neighborhood that you grew up in?

A: The neighborhood that I grew up in was a low-income neighborhood, the projects populated by blacks. One hundred percent black neighborhood. It had some violence, also drugs. It wasn't too good of a neighborhood.

Q: On your biographical form, you state that there were seven children in the family. Who raised the seven children?

A: My aunt, she raised seven of us. She had her own four children that she raised along with me, my little brother and my little sister.

Q: On your biographical form, you place her as being the most significant influence in your life. Would you speak a little bit about your aunt?

A: My aunt she is a religious person, very religious. And she stands firm in her beliefs. She was strong, and she proved that, by raising seven of us as a single parent.

Q: In order to more fully understand the environment that you grew up in, did you have to share a bedroom with any of your siblings, or cousins, in your aunt's home?

A: Yes, plenty of times. At one time, there were three of us in a room. Sometimes, I might move to one person's room, then to another person's room. That was how it was.

Q: Did you feel comfortable in those circumstances?

A: Really, I never thought about it. That's the way life was to me.

Q: Are there any poignant experiences that you would want to share regarding your foster home experiences?

A: Nothing, really. What I remember is normal, everyday stuff. Maybe just going to the store, just running in the yard. That's mainly all I could tell you.

Q: You have reached a measure of success, presently—being in college, and maintaining a good grade-point average—but how would you define "success?"

A: I feel success is not measured in dollars; I feel it is measured in attitudes and beliefs and how strong, the strength in your beliefs. That's how I feel successful is and doing the best to make yourself happy; at the same time not hurting anyone else.

Q: What would be a successful attitude?

A: A successful attitude—positive, self-esteem. You have to believe in yourself and, also, have to have a sense of education, and a sense of knowledge and wisdom.

Q: A sense of knowledge?

A: Knowledge and wisdom. Do you want me to elaborate on knowledge?

Q: OK. Can you elaborate on knowledge, then wisdom?

A: Knowledge is first of all, knowledge is know your surroundings. Be familiar with everything around you. Know your history. At the same time knowing your surroundings and your history, understanding how everything is put together. How the paths were put together. That way, it will help you towards your future.

Q: Are you relating that to the African-American experience?

A: Well, not really, but that's part of it. History could be your own family history. It doesn't have to be so general. It could be the history that you went through in your life.

Q: And wisdom. What is your definition of wisdom?

A: Wisdom is the understanding of the knowledge that you gain. That's how I define wisdom.

Q: What factors do you identify as contributing to your success?

A: I had good support from my aunt, and family; now, from my professors, but, mainly, my inner self, believing in myself, and a goal. The goal is the main factor.

Q: And what is your goal? Your most immediate goal?

A: My most immediate goal is—I want to establish myself in the black community. Really more than in the black community, but establish myself in the United States, as a prominent individual, as far as a businessmen and being involved in economics, and also in political, political situations. 'Cause I'd like to have answers to problems such as economic problems, political problems. I'd like to be a prominent figure in the United States.

Q: You'd like to be a prominent figure?

A: Yeah, become . . . yeah.

Q: What would you do if you were a prominent figure?

A: If I was a prominent figure, what I would do—as far as it goes—that would be hard to say, what I would do, because you never know how the problems, what kind of problems, you'd run into, so I can't really say what I would do—depends on what the problem is, but what I would like to do is just be there when there is a problem, and I'd like to have an answer to the problem, and if I don't have an answer, be willing to listen to whoever has the answer to the problem. That's mainly it.

Q: What kind of obstacles did you encounter to this point?

A: I was raised in a neighborhood that wasn't too positive, but I had a good aunt, who was there for me, and she supported me through the way, and she taught me right from wrong, and she put fear in my heart to make sure I do right, so really I didn't really incur any obstacles. I don't feel I have.

Q: What did you see in the neighborhood that could have impeded your progress, if you got caught up in it?

A: Violence, small gangs, and the major [one] was drugs. That was it—mainly, the drugs.

Q: And how did you avoid that kind of situation?

A: I avoided that by—if someone approached me, I would just say no to it. The reason why I would say no, not because I was afraid of the drug, but because of my aunt. Like I said, she put fear in my heart, so that's the reason, the main reason, that I kept away from drugs.

Q: What course of action would you take to overcome an obstacle that you encounter?

A: First thing, to overcome an obstacle, is just like making a decision. Decision making. First, you have to define the obstacle, analyze the obstacle, and then you have to establish alternatives to overcome the obstacle, and whichever alternatives suits you best, that's the way to go.

Q: What passes through your thoughts when you have to make a decision?

A: Main thing that comes to my thoughts is whether the decision that I'm making is right, or wrong, and who will it affect the most, and how will it affect. . . . That is what really passes through my mind.

Q: And what is inside you that motivates you to succeed?

A: Determination, positiveness, that's about it. Determination, self-esteem, and belief.

Q: And what were the major influences in your life?

A: My aunt, my family; they influenced me. Then you have the history of former black leaders like Martin Luther King and Malcolm X.

Q: Were they your role models?

A: Well, I wouldn't say they were role models, but they influenced me a lot, because of the fact that during a time when blacks were treated unfairly, they stood for what they believed in, but as far as role models, my main role model was my aunt.

Q: You noted a significant influence was your little brother. How was he an influence?

A: My little brother, mainly, because we have a very close relationship, and he's always there for me, so, in the future, I would always like to be there for him, so that's mainly the reason why he is a big influence.

Q: How much younger is he than you?

A: He's only two years younger.

Q: Is he your mother's son, as well?

A: Yes. He's my mother's son, but we don't have the same father.

Q: Did you have any teachers that influenced you?

A: Any teachers? I have a few teachers that influenced me. My twelfth-grade teacher, Mr. Gaskin, he was a black teacher, a male teacher, and he influenced me a lot, because he was always asking me where is my self-esteem, and in that way, that made me think about what was self-esteem, and try to gain it, so in that way that's how he influenced me.

Q: How did you gain it?

A: How did I gain it? I feel I gained self-esteem when I established a goal for myself, and from there, I feel I had self-esteem for myself.

Q: When you established goals, did you meet your goals?

A: Well, not as of yet, but one goal was to graduate from college, and that's what I'm in the process of doing now.

Q: Was it difficult for you to make it through high school?

A: To make it in high school, difficult? Not really, no. I really never thought of it being a problem, graduating. I just thought of it just to graduate and then just to go on to college.

Q: And what high school did you attend in Miami?

A: I attended North Miami Senior High.

Q: Were your grades good in North Miami Senior High?

A: They were average. Average.

Q: And what was your best subject in high school?

A: Math.

Q: And what is your best subject in college?

A: My best subject in college, well, it's a mixture now. I still enjoy math, but, also, I'm beginning to enjoy English and reading, which were two subjects I didn't like in high school.

Q: Did you have any peer pressure while growing up?

A: Peer pressure, yeah, I had a peer pressure, as far as dealing with drugs. I had people come to me, "Will you like to smoke a drug or deal a drug?" That's was the only peer pressure that I could remember. Really, the only peer pressure that I feel I had. Anything else wasn't too much peer pressure.

Q: How did you avoid that?

A: Like I said before, just a matter of saying no, and just thinking of the consequences of getting involved in it.

Q: Were you involved in athletics?

A: No. Not at all.

Q: How did you spend most of your time, then, other than public school, when you were growing up?

A: I spent it playing ball, laying around the house, and looking at TV, or just hanging outside and playing around.

Q: What kind of television shows did you watch when you were growing up?

A: Comedy shows and sitcoms. I mostly enjoyed comedy shows.

Q: Did you spend a lot of the time alone?

A: I would say I spent a lot of time alone.

Q: When you were young, did you attend church frequently? And what about now?

A: When we were young, we used to attend church, because my aunt used to make us, but as we got older, it became our own decision, and I decided not to go as much, like she will wish for me to go.

Q: Do you still stay in close contact with your aunt?

A: Yes. I still stay with her.

Q: Do the other children stay with her?

A: No. Only my little brother, he still stays with her.

Q: What activities do you identify as being important to your development?

A: My activities. . . . What development are you talking about?

Q: Your growth—it could be intellectual or personal growth activities.

A: Personal activities that are important—mostly, education activities, and maybe a little physical activities—that's mainly toward development.

Q: Would that be any particular sport?

A: Yeah, the particular sport, I would say, would be football.

Q: What organizations do you belong to that help you develop?

A: Really, I wasn't involved in organizations, not until the age of sixteen, that's when I participated in park activities and playing tennis. That was my first participation in an organization activity.

Q: Did you go away to summer camp when you were a youth?

A: No, I never went away.

Q: What did you do in the summer?

A: In the summer, I just mainly hung around, hung with some guys and go out to the park and play.

Q: You've been accepted into The President's Men program this year. What do you look forward to in that program?

A: I look forward to being more active in community services, and I also look forward to being more active in school activities. That's what I look forward to.

Q: I see on your biographical profile that you don't belong to a fraternity. You don't wish to belong to a fraternity?

A: It's not that I don't really wish not to be part of a fraternity 'cause sometimes I have mixed feelings on, "Should I, or should I not." I really don't think about it too much.

Q: You don't feel a sense of being left out—others belong and you do not belong?

A: No. I don't.

Q: Do you have close friends on the campus?

A: Yeah. I have close friends. The closest friend is my friend, E. She's the closest friend I've got, and my roommate [not on campus]. That's the closest friends I got.

Q: Do you live on the campus most of the time during the week?

A: Yeah.

Q: And how do you spend your time?

A: I spend it. . . . I try to spend the majority of it studying and preparing myself for schoolwork, and I spend it sometimes with my friend, E, and I also try to spend some time in SGA [Student Government Association] because I am part of the SGA, and the rest of the time, just leisure time, maybe just laying down looking at TV, or playing basketball or playing a video game.

Q: Are you very involved in the SGA?

A: Yes. Very involved in it.

Q: What do you actually do?

A: My title is a comptroller, but it is the same as being a treasurer, so my responsibility is keeping the records of all expenditures. I keep the budget of the SGA. That's my main responsibility.

Q: How many hours a week do you put into that task?

A: I'd say about ten to fifteen hours per week.

Q: Do you have work?

A: Yes, I have a job.

Q: What is your job?

A: I work at UPS as a loader.

Q: How many hours a week do you work at UPS?

A: I work about twenty to twenty-five hours a week.

Q: When do you go to work?

A: I go to work at 10:30 to 2:30, sometimes it may extend to 3:00.

Q: Is it 10:30 P.M.?

A: P.M.

Q: Are you saying that you don't get home until 3:00 A.M. in the morning?

A: Yes.

Q: That sounds like a difficult responsibility—working and keeping up with schoolwork.

A: Yes, it is.

Q: Do you have any message that you would like to share with young black males in the community?

A: I'd tell them to try and set a goal in life, because that's the most important thing in life, and define a purpose, and I'd also tell them to take life easy. Whatever life give hard, just take it easy. That would be the best way to do life. Set a goal, and define a purpose towards your goal.

Q: And can you give an example of what you mean by taking life easy?

A: Well, it means by taking life easy . . . gaining knowledge and wisdom and, also, at the same time, having a lot of patience, that way when situations comes up, you'll be able to understand the problem, figure out the problem. When you have the patience, along with the understanding, I think that helps to take life much more easy . . . not to worry about too many problems, because if you begin to worry, that's the wrong route to take, and the problems just get worse. Don't worry, stay cool, and calm, understand the problem, figure out the problem.

Q: Is that how you get through each day?

A: Yeah. Most of the time.

Q: Do you have any significant worries?

A: My major significant worry right now is trying to do the best I can in school. That's my most significant worry right now.

Q: What part does E play in your life?

A: Seriously. She is a good support. She supports me; she's my girlfriend. She's there when she sees me being too laid back, and she's there to try and push me, and that's good.

Q: Did you meet her at college?

A: Yeah.

Q: You say that you've been inspired and motivated by your teachers. Are you speaking about the teachers in this college?

A: Yeah. I'm talking about the General Study teachers and teachers in the Business Department.

Q: Could you give examples of how they have inspired and motivated you?

A: Many of the teachers they show that they really care about their students, and I have received many statements that they really do care about their students. There is one particular teacher that is always checking on my grades, and that shows to me that he really cares, and he comes up to me and tells me, and when he sees that I'm not doing very well, he comes up to me, and says, "You're not doing too well," and that shows he cares. And other teachers, who spend time in between their lecture or talking, they may get off the subject, and try to help other students out by telling them the situation in the United States ain't too good, and it's up to us to try and make it different, so they might slip off their discussion that they planned to talk about, to inspire the students to be more active in their studies.

Q: Can you more fully share with young black males your ideas for achieving "success?"

A: For a black male to be successful, you have to try and find out what's the problem, and then try a stronger approach to education, much more stern education, more discipline. I feel that education is more like a training program, rather than an education. They don't teach us; they don't reach to the psychological matters; they just stay on the basics: math, English, and history, and I feel they should go into more psychological matters about the environment, and, I feel, that that's the emphasis we have to give it. And, also, we have to have a goal. As the people, black males, we have to have a goal in life and that's mainly it.

Q: When you say "psychological factors about the environment," what does that mean?

A: I mean we need to be taught about more situations in the community. How does a community establish factors, such as, as far as family factors. I can't really express what I want to say, but how families are put together. They got to be taught more about customs in our communities. Because in college, we talk about man in society, sociology, but in high school, we're not taught anything about that—we're just taught about history, and math, and English, which is good, but we need to know about sociology areas.

Q: While growing up in a predominantly all-black neighborhood, were you able to see beyond your immediate surroundings?

A: It distracted me as far as my relationship with other races, because all I saw was my community; it also affected me in relationships with higher-income black communities and that's really how it affected me and my understanding of other people—a difference of circumstances.

Q: When you were growing up in a predominantly black neighborhood, did you envision yourself "getting out" and going to college?

A: I always envisioned myself going to college and to really get out of that kind of environment, and I just say, "It was bad"—not too bad, but a negative neighborhood— but I just felt that it wasn't positive enough, and I looked at the fact that my aunt, she went through a lot in raising us and trying to go to school at the same time, and going to work, that's all she could manage, staying in that kind of income neighborhood. That was another factor, 'cause I saw that she worked very hard, and I could tell that she wasn't happy where she was at, and that it wasn't too good of a place. More reason to inspire me to try and help myself to move out of that neighborhood.

Q: To more fully obtain some insight into your home environment in the Overtown project—having seven children in the dwelling—would you relate the number of bedrooms in the apartment?

A: At first, we had three bedrooms and one den, then we moved to a five-bedroom apartment, which was more comfortable.

Q: When you go back to the neighborhood now—a senior student in college—do you see things differently?

A: I don't go back too much. Maybe once in awhile, then I might meet some people who I grew up with, or who are new, who still stay in that neighborhood, and I ask questions, and what I found different was the attitude of the younger generation. The younger generation is more violent and their attitude is more negative then when I was growing up. When I was growing up, there wasn't too much talk about shooting someone, or robbing somebody. There wasn't too much disrespect for the elderly. When I was growing up, we had more respect for the elders than they do today, in my neighborhood. And, also, my neighborhood is more infested by drugs than it was when I was growing up.

Q: Are there gangs now?

A: Well, it hasn't yet become a gang neighborhood. When I was growing up, it was small gangs. Today, the gangs in the neighborhood, they deal in drugs. It's not like an organized gang. The core of the gangs is their relationship with the drug business.

Q: Did you experience any of the riots?

A: Yeah.

Q: Where were you at the time?

A: At the time, I was just around the house at the time. I was just running around. I was young, I was just running around. I mainly stayed in the house, but it was outside, but I saw everything that was going on. I saw the neighborhood.

Q: Did you feel a lot of fear?

A: Fear. No. I didn't feel no fear. It was just to me people running around. To me, it was just fun. I didn't see any harm in it. I knew it was violence, but it wasn't no violence in the neighborhood. It was outside the neighborhood. So, mainly, I thought it was fun.

Q: What do you think about it now, in retrospect?

A: Thinking back, I think now of it as more of a serious situation. I see how it affected neighborhoods. I see that now. When they was doing that, all they was doing was destroying their own neighborhood. That's how I look at it now.

Q: What would you say to the young people who are perhaps frustrated and would get involved like that again? What would you say to them now?

A: I tell them if you want to make a change, violence is unnecessary, is not the way to do it. If you want to make a change, you have to establish yourselves as a people, as a group, and organize yourself, and make a better approach, as far as politically trying to make a difference, instead of randomly trying to make one.

*   *   *

Respondent was asked to write down additional comments (after interview was transcribed) in order to obtain more information in regard to the following:

Research Question #6: What are the reasons why the activities and organizations that you participated in (including athletics) were/are important to you?

A: I played tennis in a summer program at my neighborhood park. I wanted to be active in a sport, and because there was no organized football team, I selected to play tennis. The purpose—to be actively involved in an organized sport was to occupy my time and to be part of something that I like. In high school, I went out for the football team, but I did not follow through with the decision. My pursuit was intervened by my aunt who did not want me to play. She thought that I would get injured, because I was very skinny. I wanted to play football, because it was always my childhood dream. I loved the game, and I wanted to fulfill that desire.

I decided to come to college to better myself, socially and to upgrade my educational level. During high school, I rarely thought of entering the college level, because I figured that after graduation, I could find a nice-paying job easily. But after graduation, the experience that followed proved to me otherwise. The nice-paying job never came, and, basically, I was "dead." The experience proved that I needed a higher form of education, and/or vocational skills. I chose education.

I decided to be a member of the SGA cabinet, because I wanted to be involved with something that was important on the campus. I figured that being part of the SGA, I would gain an important position and experience towards my major.

OBSERVER'S COMMENTS

Respondent:
- is 5 feet, 11 inches, 150 pounds;
- is quiet, reserved, describes self as "laid back";
- picks friends carefully, observes person first to determine what he has in common with the person;

- in order to get friendly, he would have to relate in the "same" direction;
- if the respondent sees any "negativeness," he withdraws; "negativeness" would mean smoking and/or stealing drugs, talking about violence, "using" people;
- gets more talkative when knowing and accepting the person, but "not too talkative";
- is a good listener; "I'll listen to the person, never make a judgment"; will think about what he heard—"conservative";
- doesn't like to be in the "spotlight"; doesn't like to "praise himself";
- doesn't feel comfortable in others praising him, will try to reject it (modest).

INTERVIEW 25

Q: Could you describe the home that you grew up in?

A: Well, basically, the home that I grew up in was in the project area of Liberty City—right off of 62nd Street.

Q: Was it an apartment?

A: They were project HUD [U.S. Department of Housing and Urban Development]—you can call them apartments. They were basically HUD homes.

Q: Is the correct spelling "H-U-D?"

A: Correct.

Q: Could you describe the inside of your home?

A: The inside of our home was very clean, because we had to keep it that way. We had no other choice. My mom was a very clean lady. She always forced us to make sure the house was clean all the time, so I would say the inside of our house was always clean. Regardless of the outside, we always made the inside look good.

Q: How many bedrooms did you have in that HUD apartment?

A: It was a two-bedroom.

Q: On your biographical sheet, you note that you have four brothers; did you have to share a room or a bed with any of your brothers?

A: In the past, what we did was, my mom had a room, and the brothers—all of us was in one room. We had bunk beds, so it was easy for us—two and two.

Q: Could you describe the environment outside the home in your neighborhood?

A: The environment outside was a little bit different. You had some who cared about the community, and, then, you also had the others who do not care about the community, and it was very violent as far as hearing bullets being fired all the time—you know— you're constantly getting into a lot of fights. It was just violence. I wouldn't say every day, but the majority of the time, it was basically violent.

Q: How did you survive?

A: Well, my mom was very strict with us as far as going outside and playing and engaging in—getting into crowds. So we, the majority of the time, stayed at home, and while we were at home, we would always tend to our school work and, then, when we do go outside, we go outside where we were right in front of the house and play football, and just play out in the little parking area that they had, so most of the time was spent in the home to try and get through the violence that was outside.

Q: Was there anything that touched upon you directly?

A: The thing that—no, not really, because I am one who cares about my school work, and even at that age, I still cared about my school work, and I cared about where I stood in school, as far as test scores. I was one who cared about that—my GPA, so not really. My schoolwork really touched me a lot.

Q: Do you focus mostly on your schoolwork?

A: Yes, I do.

Q: What public schools did you attend while you were growing up in that area?

A: Martin Luther King Elementary School, Holmes Elementary School, Charles R. Drew Junior High, and Miami Northwestern Senior High School.

Q: Could you tell us what factors contributed to your success?

A: Teachers, the majority, teachers, watching them, listening to them—basically, all teachers. You know, I get motivated off of teachers because of the fact that they encourage me to do my best, and they make sure of it. They force me—I shouldn't say they force, but they make sure I get the job done, and I am really grateful towards teachers.

Q: Are these male or female teachers?

A: Both.

Q: Could you give an example of some teacher that stands out in your mind and what they did to motivate you?

A: There are so many of them. Just to mention one, I would actually have to say Dr. H, which is the math teacher at Miami Northwestern Senior High School. What Dr. H did—I had Dr. H during my sophomore year in high school and then I felt the need—I said, "This guy is great. I have to take him again," so I took him for my junior and my senior year. And for a person that is really confused when it comes to math, he stayed there, he kept me after school, and he even kept me to his class after the class was over with. If he knew, like for instance PE—that was really irrelevant—so he would write me a pass, because he wanted to make sure that I learned my math—just the integrity that he has. He pushed me to do my best—self-motivation.

Q: Are you saying that he served as your role model, as well as mentor?

A: Yes, he did.

Q: Were you involved in athletics when you were growing up?

A: No, I wasn't.

Q: Your main focus, then, was on academics?

A: It was on academics. I also took some work on extra-curricular.

Q: What were those extra-curricular activities?

A: Well, in high school, I was the student government vice president, student government president, and, also, the district student government president for Dade County public schools.

Q: Can you identify reasons for your involvement?

A: Well, in the past, Northwestern has been noted for a lot of violence taking place, as far as guns being in schools, drugs being in schools, and, basically, I felt the need to go back to the tradition. And the tradition was to start getting Northwestern acting on a more academic standpoint and start bringing the media out to show that Northwestern is not all about violence all the time. We're a bunch of students that are concerned about education and feel the need for education. And the tradition was to bring them back to where our forefathers—where are parents were when they graduated from the halls of Miami Northwestern. And that's what we focused on as president and as vice president of the Student Government Association at Miami Northwestern. Our goal was to bring back the education, or responsibility, towards Miami Northwestern and towards our students, and we did accomplish that.

Q: What course of action did you take to overcome the obstacles that you encountered?

A: Various tutoring sessions, since we have the—I believe it was the Compact program that was coming in—the Magnet program that was coming into our schools. We used various tutoring sessions where we stayed after school. Teachers stayed after school to help tutor for the SAT [Scholastic Aptitude Test] and the ACT [American College Testing examination]. Then, we also had the Saturday classes where our students were asked to come, and we had the majority of them that did, to get help with their SAT and ACT. We, also, had various reading programs. During our homerooms, we would take fifteen minutes and read whatever you like—in a magazine, a regular book, or even just whatever your teacher assigned, you know, novels or whatever. We had various reading sessions. We constantly did—gave out little incentives for academics contests we had, such as Brain Bowls and things of that nature. So, we really pushed for academics during those two years.

Q: Were you working with a group of youngsters, or particular youngsters, in these activities?

A: I was working with a group of youngsters—well—they were working with me to help the whole school. So, I don't want to limit it to just—let's say—fifteen people. It was working with, basically, the whole school. What we did was—we got in contact with all the teachers. And this was a project for the whole entire school—it was mandatory—fifteen minutes for every class. Every teacher who had a homeroom had to conduct their class during the fifteen minutes of the reading time, and with the tutoring sessions for the SAT and the ACT—it was just a toss-up. Anyone who wanted to come, ninth graders included, since SAT and ACT is really not required until the junior year, but we had tenth graders that was getting interested in that, so, we threw it at everybody, and everybody took part.

Q: Why are these activities important to you—what kind of feelings did you get on the inside in helping?

A: Well, when it was time to go, it made me cry. So, tears came to the eyes—so I can really say I got a good feeling from it—you know—just me helping others, and I think doing that is really what kept me—what keeps me motivated, especially since I've been at this college, because now I am able to do the same thing, and it was just great. I liked it a lot.

Q: You noted on your biographical sheet that you are involved in the student government organization on this campus. What is your role?

A: Student Government Activities Director, and I am, also, the sophomore class president.

Q: Do you act as a role model and mentor here, as well?

A: Yes, I do. For example, it's just what I have in my hand now. Next week, we're going to Miami Northwestern Senior High School, and we are going to have a Christmas program to conduct for five hundred elementary school students, both from Miami—from Holmes Elementary and Martin Luther King, Jr., Elementary.

Q: What factors contributed to your success in your life?

A: Watching others, especially right now, since I have my internship—watching a lot of the judges, and seeing which role they play—seeing how they can be able to hear two sides and just come up with one big decision—people from my job, as well.

Q: What reasons can you identify for the importance of "watching others"?

A: When I see individuals that are doing extremely well, and you know that they come from a background that was out of the ordinary, was low—you know—low income in the family, brothers and sisters was on drugs and just them overcoming that obstacle, and be able to go all the way, that really pushes me. Work, school, my family, WT, who is the new senator of District 37, I believe, and Judge CM. These are the type of people that push me and motivate me to keep going.

Q: You said on your biographical form that your grandparents, both grandmother and grandfather, were involved 80 percent of the time in your upbringing. Could you talk about them?

A: They definitely helped to motivate me, because I tell you, whenever you can't—do something wrong—then it's time to run, because they just bring out everything. They fuss at you. It's just the constant fussing, and, I guess, when you get tired of people fussing at you all the time for doing something wrong, you know that it is time to make a change and that's what my grandmother, even my grandfather, even my mother, fussed at me a lot when I was at the young stage, because of the things that I did wrong. And it's not until—it wasn't until my ninth grade year that I really said, "It is time to change; it's time to take a turn, and really start reaching for something more positive and not negative all the time." My grandmother and my grandparents—they definitely did a lot—a lot of fussing, a lot of running after me. They helped a lot within the family. They really did.

Q: When you said you took a turn—from where to where?

A: Well, I guess, although I was doing good "schoolwise," but still, it's the crowd that you hang around with, and with some of my friends, I was constantly getting into fights. I never got into any major trouble, like ever going to jail or anything of that nature, or rob. That was insufficient to me. But as far as getting into a lot of fights, miscellaneous arguments, things like that—that was really my problem—talking back, because I had low patience—and, now, I am able to control, to be able to control things in a minute, you know, regardless of the situation. I can more humble myself compared to then. So, that's what I mean when we're talking a turnaround.

Q: What factors do you identify that could have been obstacles to your success?

A: Well, the biggest—well—as I look at it, it's just, basically, my lack of patience, because I have low patience, and it was like whenever somebody either said something about my mom, or said something about anybody in my family, or anything that was derogatory to me, I'd just snap, you know, without even thinking. Now I am able to just hear a person, let them say whatever they want to say, and take it, because I know that they're no better than me, I'm no better than them, but I know that I can move on to higher grounds, and because of what they are doing at that point is very insufficient, and I don't have to stoop to their level to do so. So, it's just, basically, controlling myself. Now, I have gathered patience among myself and being more humbled.

Q: Who taught you to be humble and have patience?

A: Once again, that's where we go back to Dr. H. I guess, he learned from how he puts it, "It's good when you are in fraternity." And fraternity, he said, would definitely teach you that. That is something else. I couldn't be able to vouch for that, but just listening to him, and him being able to control me in the past, is really what helped me out, so he really helped with the patience part, because my mom used to say all the time, "You have short patience. That's why I be on you all the time. And you sit up here, and you talk back to me," this and that. You know, I guess I get tired of her fussing, so that plays a part, too, but Dr. H really helped me out, as well.

Q: What organizations can you identify as being important to your continuing development?

A: Student government.

Q: Why reasons can you identify for its importance?

A: Because of the fact that it teaches me constitutional grounds. I have to make sure—it teaches me networking with both students and networking with faculty, and even networking with the community. So, I would say student government.

Q: Both on a public school level and a college level?

A: Yes.

Q: What has been your role in The President's Men organization?

A: At this point, with The President's Men, we really just, basically, are coming up with ideas, trying to help improve the college, me working with P as the SGA vice president, and I am the SGA Activities Director, just working together, to try and make improvements towards the school in where students can feel comfortable here, so that they don't want to leave, where our retention rate will remain high, and just doing—helping the school out, and doing whatever we can that's necessary, both school and community.

Q: How are you involved in the community, presently?

A: Well, I started a program in high school called "The New Generation," and that program focused towards elementary school students—fourth-graders at the time. And I went out to the Charles R. Drew Elementary School, and I taught from, basically, a manual that I had a long time ago—leadership abilities, leadership—how to resolve conflict without resulting into violence. And, at this point in time, to keep that up, what I am planning on doing, and what I'm doing now, is still constantly going out to elementary schools, and do the same thing, or if not that subject, just doing on other subjects like for instance, on December 9th, our program—the theme is putting students first in the pursuit of excellence.

Q: What emphasis do you place on these types of community activities?

A: The topic that we want our guest speaker to speak on would be developing dreams and making them come true. We want them to be able to dream and see that those dreams can one day come true only if they reach for it, and you have to be able to take a stand, reach for it, and then, finally, go for it. You know, just because you are reaching, just doesn't mean you are going to actually get it. You have to be able to go for it. You have to put in the time, put in the service, whatever is needed for you to reach your goal, and be able to grasp it—so that's basically it.

Q: What strategies do you use, personally, to reach your goals, or to overcome obstacles?

A: The strategies I use—I guess you can say when—by me being employed with the Dade County Courthouse, and that requires me to go into the Dade County Jail a lot, and just the look, looking around, it's a place where you don't feel comfortable, and it's a place where you definitely don't want to be in the future, and when I see what can happen if I was ever to take the negative route, and I shouldn't say "if," because there will be no "if" on this part, but just to see what others are going through at this time, just because they have taken the negative road. And I am very surprised—though on Sundays, when I walk in the Dade County Jail, and I see so many of the defendants that have taken a turn—they know they can't get out, but they have changed their lifestyles. They are in the church service that is normally held every Sunday in the Dade County Jail. And talking with some of them is very interesting, as well. I guess seeing—how can I put this—seeing what can, could happen to me in the future, if I was to ever go down a negative road—the places I don't want to be—I guess, your visualization on that—that's a tough question. I guess, by me visualizing them, and seeing the predicament that they're in at this point, I know I would never want to be there, so that definitely has to make me push forward, to make sure I do what I have to do to stay on the outside, and not, you know, be incarcerated or anything of that nature.

Q: On your biographical sheet, you noted that religion is not applicable. Could you explain your feelings on religion?

A: I figured my—I say to myself, I am agnostic, and that is an individual who believes in a Supreme Being, but yet does not take sides. I can't ever walk up to a Muslim, and say that his religion is false. I can't walk up to a Jewish person, and say that his religion is false, and I can't walk up to a Catholic, and say their religion is false. Every religion has different meanings, different styles. One of them could be true, but, then again, if one of them is true, then you have so many other different religions that are not true. And you don't know which one is true, so I tend not to take sides. I acknowledge that there is a Supreme Being that placed us on this earth, and gives us the power to breathe on this earth, every day, and I acknowledge that there is a God somewhere, but yet, I don't want to take sides, and say whose religion is false, whose religion is not false, because that's not my place to do so. Like I said earlier, I can't say that what Muslims say about Mohammed is a lie. I can't say what Christians feel about Jesus Christ is a lie, and I can't say what the Buddhists, or what Jews—you know, I don't want to take sides, because religion is a subject that's very—I wouldn't say complicated, but it is very contradictory, because you don't know which one to believe, whose telling the truth, so I try not take sides in religion. I go to church. I go to a Baptist church, you know, because you still have to have religion a part of you, okay. I go there just, basically, to realize that there is a Supreme Being who placed us on this earth, but I don't want to take sides.

Q: How often do you go to the church?

A: Because of my involvement in work, I try and go at least twice a month, but I have to go to the night service, because we do have jail arraignments during the morning sessions, and that's during church.

Q: Let us return to discussing your internship. Does it involve the jail program that you are speaking about?

A: Yes, it does. The internship is wonderful. As a matter of fact, by me being a computer science/criminal justice major, a lot of people used to say, "K, you like to debate a lot, so you should be a lawyer." I said, "No," that's too long of school for me. But, then again, you know, like the phrase goes, "Hard work pays off," and I sit in the courtroom, and I see the judge, I see the state attorneys, the public defenders, and I see the wonderful job that they do, and I know I like to debate, so that's a position where I would want to be. And what really motivates me to go to higher grounds to the judgeship is due to the fact of our lack of minorities, blacks, particularly, within the ranks of becoming a judge. As I was speaking to a judge yesterday morning—Sunday—and she was telling me that herself, which is Judge MG, and Judge TT, were the only two black women judges there were—I guess within their specific division—I don't know—within Dade County. But, since I have been working at the internship, there has only been two African-American women that I've seen, and only one African-American male. And as I was talking to her, it was interesting, because she said that there are three others. There is Judge WF; there is Judge CM; there is LA, and there is another judge by the last name of Judge P. I don't know his first name. But, you figure—you know—out of all the blacks, all the African Americans that go to law school, all the African Americans that we have, males in particular, there should be more within our judicial system. I figure, I don't like to sit down and complain all the time. If I'm going to sit down and complain, then I might as well do something about it. And the only way to do something about it is to get involved in the system that controls it. And that's what I figured. That's what I want to do in my life. Yes, the system has—I wouldn't say it goes against African Americans constantly—that I wouldn't say, because that would be a very racial statement, but if so many blacks have complaints about our judicial system, then they need to get in, and do something about it, and that's what I want to do. I want to be able to make sure that justice is served for everybody. And just watching them, and talking with her yesterday, Judge MG, that talk really motivated me, to say, I know that our judicial system needs some work and has to change, and the only way you're going to change is if you get in there and do something about it, and that's why my desire is to be a county judge and hopefully go farther. That's why I decided to do it. I feel as though I'm going to get in the system, and I'm going to do my best to make a change.

Q: How are you going to do that? What strategy are you going to use to get into the system.

A: Starting now, being educated and going to school. Once I graduate from—I don't know if I'm going to stay at this college, but for law school, I will be going, and, hopefully, I'll make it—if God allows, to Georgetown University. From Georgetown University, then I plan to go into practice as a state attorney, or a district attorney. And from there, just go up the ladder. You know, you have to start at the bottom and work your way up. So, I plan on starting as a state prosecutor and hopefully, by doing a good thing there, I'm going to evaluate myself for ten years as a state attorney, before I decide to move on up the ladder to becoming a judge.

Q: How do you define success?

A: I define success as one who is able to reach their goals that they had all along. In other words, at this point in time, by me being a sophomore in college—a first-semester sophomore—I'm saying my goal is to become a county judge, a state attorney first, then a county judge, within my criminal justice career and my law career, or if I decide to go in my computer career, then I would rather be a systems analyst. Those are my goals, now. Success happens when you accomplish those goals. You know that you have laid out your yellow brick road. You know you have to end where you want to be. And if you reach there, you know, it's not going to be easy. Of course, you are going to have those hard obstacles to cross, and if you just reach there, if you just touch it, grasp and get it, then I feel as though that's success—being able to overcome various things to reach your goals. That's success.

Q: What motivates you? What drives you?

A: Once again, we look at—I would say—first of all, my family. Then I would say my school, because like they say, "Hard work does pay off," and it all comes back to you in the end. And, then, when I look at the judges, and I talk to some of the judges—they are very motivating. And, then, I guess, my involvement with the Student Government Association. That's very—in getting out into the community, being able to interact with some of the youngsters. That's very motivating for me. As a matter of fact, that's the number one priority. That's why I continue to do it. That's, basically, it. My family—you know—it's in my heart. It's in my heart.

Q: What goes through your thoughts when you have to make a decision?

A: Oh, a lot, because when you make a decision, as far as on a big decision at that, you have to wonder. You know you're not—you know everybody is not going to respect the decision that you make, but then again, you know there will be some who will respect the decision. So, you can't take sides. You have to always stay neutral. And the thoughts, it'll give you a headache. Trust me, it'll give you a headache, because I know I've gotten headaches off of some. Some of the decisions that I've made as an activities director, or even as a class president, or as a student government president in the past, I have to hold off to delay those decisions to probably a week or two, because you really have to look at the situation. But, the first thing that goes through my mind is—I have to gather facts. I have to have evidence on whatever the decision may be, evidence of statistics, whatever. But, I look at factual information and just go from there. You know, I survey students, survey others, and see how they feel, and then, basically, off of their remarks, I just go from there.

Q: You noted on your biographical sheet that your mother and family have been the most influential in your life. Could you explain further?

A: Well, first of all, if it wasn't for my mother, I wouldn't be here. And if it definitely wasn't for my father, I wouldn't be here. And, then, if it wasn't for the motivation coming from the family in its entirety—on my mom's side—that's one thing I need to acknowledge more specifically—on my mom's side. With my mom's determination, as far as when I look at the past with my mom, my mom didn't graduate from high school. She completed just up to her senior year, and, really, all her life is, basically, work, work, work, work, work for the family. And looking at how she can overcome a struggle, without even having a high school diploma, you know, it's been very motivating for me although I—she, she pushes us. She would make sure we cannot come in her house without a high school diploma. So, that's one thing that really motivates us. We know what we have to bring in—in order to stay there, but it's just her integrity, her determination, her perseverance, and her character. Those are the key elements that played a very important part in my life, that really has me to push forth, and to do both—help individuals within the school and help individuals within the community.

Q: Could you talk about what your father's role has been?

A: At this point in time, I can really say up to my fifth grade, my father's role was just that—a father. You know, he helped me out. He didn't stay with us at the time, but you know, still, he'd come over, he'd make sure my education—he stayed on me with my books. As a matter of fact, whenever I had a problem with education—like talking back to a teacher, or just grades were down, and things like that—the first person my mom called was my father. I knew it was time to either start hiding under a bed or do something. But he has definitely stayed on me when he was there, in reference to my education and social things. Whenever, I needed something, he was there. I'd asked him, and he would give. So, I never had a problem, you know, with my father.

Q: Was he in the home as you were growing up?

A: No. He wasn't in the home.

Q: How did he make his living?

A: He owned, as a matter of fact, he owned two beauty salons. He is a beautician. They used to call it "Razzmatazz"—one in Coconut Grove, and one in the Liberty City area. So that's how he earned his living. He was a good—he's okay—he had his own business, and he helped everyone out.

Q: You are the oldest—but did you have any significant input from your younger brothers regarding your own life?

A: Well, I, because of their age, I really couldn't say, "Yes," because it's basically me who had to do all the work and had to give the motivation around the house when it comes to them. They see how me, and my other brother, worked together—he does his "thing" as far as community work is concerned. As a matter of fact, recently, he just finished working with FW, DS, and even when [actor] Danny Glover was in town—so he had done a lot—he's done his part. He's still in high school, about to graduate, and just, basically, my little brothers look at both of us—look at the things that we do.

Q: Did you have peer group influence?

A: No. Everything was just done by networking. You have to talk to a lot of people to see what they have been through and, you know, just for you to visualize what you have to come to in the near future, so just, basically, networking, talking to various people, is really what motivated me. I never—because, I guess, I hate being involved in real groups—I guess sitting in—I don't even like to attend meetings, and I'm the president of things. I don't like calling meetings, because I don't like sitting in one room, or one big area for a while. You know, I just like single-handedly networking with individuals, talking to them about their background, and educational backgrounds that they have.

Q: When you were growing up, people your own age—your peers—did they influence you?

A: I guess people my age—I would have to say, "No," they didn't. The only individual that did would be RD. And R, his mom definitely stayed on him to make sure he didn't go outside. He didn't do anything. He had to make sure he stayed in his books, and you can see where that all paid off, because, finally, we both graduated from the same high school together, and R graduated valedictorian. So, and he also received the Harvard Book, which is a very prestigious book, that they give to the individual student in high school with the highest GPA, and his GPA was over a 4.0, so his hard work did pay off—definitely.

Q: What would you say to young black men in the community? What message would you give them?

A: Just what I have down here—putting students first in the pursuit of excellence. I have to get them to realize that academics is their number one, and should remain their number one priority at this stage in life. You cannot bypass education. When you go to a job, the first thing they are going to ask you is about your education. I don't care if it's Burger King. If it is Burger King, you have to know how to work a machine. You have to know how to add and subtract. You have to know how to do math and everything. When you go to retail stores, you have to know how to present yourselves, accordingly, in the front of customers. You have to—your appearance, your communication skills, as far as in reference to customer service—so, I would really get them—I would let them know that education is number one, and it should remain number one for the rest of their lives, especially during this critical point in time. We have a lot of young African Americans that are going to jail over various amounts of reasons, and they have to see that that's not the place where they should be. They should be in the school with the book in their hands learning. Not in school with a gun in their hand, looking for someone else to be their next victim.

OBSERVER'S COMMENTS

Respondent:
- is extremely "busy," almost always "in motion";
- walks fast, in an extreme hurry to get things done;
- with his philosophy of placing excellence first, and his ability to get involved in beneficial community services, he tends to stand out as a caring person with great potential to fulfill his dreams.

INTERVIEW 27

Q: Could you describe the home you grew up in?

A: I basically grew up in a middle-class neighborhood—not too much crime around the area—a nice house—a family of just my mother, my sister, my brother and my niece and nephew. That's about it.

Q: How many rooms did you have in your home?

A: Three rooms.

Q: And did you have to share a bedroom with . . . ?

A: I shared first with my brother, and then with my nephew.

Q: Could you describe the neighborhood environment?

A: Peaceful. The neighborhood we had a lot of immigrants coming in—Jamaicans, and stuff like that. So, it was like a mixed culture. We had some Caucasians, and so it was nice. It was a nice neighborhood.

Q: And what section of Miami do you live in?

A: Carol City.

Q: Can you describe your peer groups when you were growing up?

A: The peer groups when I grew up—they was a conservative group of people. We all knew exactly what we wanted to get out of life. A few of my friends went the wrong way, but it's not that they was originally bad, they just, more or less, wanted to be bad, wanted to have guns, and wanted to do this, and I kinda steered away from that. I didn't have a lot of friends. It was mostly just me and my dog, basically.

Q: How did you stay away? What strategy did you use, or action did you use to stay away?

A: Fortunately, my friends that did steer on the wrong side, they never pressured me. I never was put under peer pressure. They did what they did, and, in fact, most of them decided to do what they did at a later time in life—elementary, they were good students, and everything. And, let's say, I spent most of my time in the fields just running with my dog. I didn't have a lot, lot of friends.

Q: What other activities were you involved in in growing up?

A: Track and field. I played football a couple of years. That's about it—exercise and karate.

Q: Which activity were you most involved in?

A: Track and field.

Q: Are you still involved in track and field?

A: No. It's kind of hard with college going on. I tend to be out of shape.

Q: What factors do you identify as contributing to your success?

A: I guess I have to say sitting around the home and knowing my mother, who works as a housemaid, working hard, and didn't make a great deal of money, but we didn't know that because she always would buy our clothes for us. We never went out without clothes. I can wear something one Monday and wouldn't have to wear it for the next two weeks. She always looked out for us, always constantly working around the house, never sat down, and although she worked hard, I felt that in order to get what I wanted, I would have to work hard. But I wouldn't do what she was doing.

Q: Is she a role model for you in any way?

A: Yes, Yes. She—just going after what you want, and not waiting around, and seeing what's gonna happen, and let the world fly you by, and not waiting on anybody to do anything for you. She went after what she got. She made the money that she needed. She provided for us—and she is doing that today.

Q: Did you have a relationship with your father?

A: I saw him every two weeks. We tend to speak a little more now, but it wasn't more than him just bringing over the money, and that was it—a couple of broken promises, but I'm over that now.

Q: Did he ever stay in the house with you?

A: Not since I was three years old when they moved from Overtown, 'cause they originally lived on 7th Court, where the Arena is presently at now. Then we moved over.

Q: Could you give us your definition for success?

A: Success is achieving—reaching the ultimate goal—your goal of not just financial, but being with a nice house, a nice family and a nice job that you feel comfortable doing, not one that you're stuck in for the money, or anything like that—but one that you really enjoy doing—and helping people.

Q: Did you have any obstacles that could have prevented you from getting to this point in your life?

A: No, not too many. Other than just trying to stay away from those that was doing wrong, I didn't really have too many obstacles.

Q: How did you occupy yourself or what thoughts pass through your mind when you had to make an important decision like staying away from your peer group that you didn't care for?

A: As I stated earlier, basically, seeing my mother working hard, working hard for whatever she got, never seeing anything coming easy. I mean, you work hard, and keeping to myself, mostly. I did a lot of growing up, I did a lot of excess amounts of exercise, like I said, going out into the fields, being with my dog. And I spent most of maybe 70 percent/80 percent of the time, just me and my dog in a quiet place, just thinking about where I wanted to be ten to twenty years from now, and not letting anything get in my way.

Q: Could you talk about the influences in your life, starting with your family?

A: Well, my family, my mother played the head role in the house. Like I said, she provided what she could. She showed us right from wrong. She instilled it in us. My sister, more or less, was—she was, in her own way, a special person. She did a lot for us. She made more money, so she can provide that social aspect, as far as going out, going on vacations and stuff like that—buying x amount of clothes. As far as my teachers, my teachers just made sure I did—I was doing my work when it needed to be done.

Q: Were there any teachers that stand out in your mind?

A: Mrs. C, she was my first grade and my third grade teacher. She taught us a lot. When I see kids growing up now in the first grade, they not getting the same kind of education I got. I mean, she made sure we knew [our] home address, and all kinds of stuff like this. And back then, it was discipline in the elementary schools, which I think is the great reason why they are going the way they are now—from a lack of discipline.

Q: Who impressed you with discipline?

A: Mrs. C, although she kept a mutual relationship with my mother, because she lived like three houses down. I don't know, maybe 'cause she was my first-grade teacher, I'll just never forget her. She did a lot.

Q: And the church—did the church influence your life?

A: We went to church occasionally, and the church didn't really do too much for me.

Q: What other role models would you have, for instance, in the community, or in athletics, or in college?

A: In the community, more or less, I guess firefighters and police officers going out there, knowing that—I feel like being a police officer you come constantly face-to-face with death, and you do not know once you leave the house whether you'll come back the next day or night. I mean, it just takes a lot of courage to do that, and everybody's not on your side, so credit should be due them. As far as college, I think my biggest role model is my new adopted family, the "Alphas" [Alpha Phi Alpha fraternity]. I mean, I'm surrounded by people anywhere from thirty years old to my age, which is nineteen, that make good grades—they know what they're after. We're role models in the community, we're all on campus and everything, and, I mean, that's who I really look up to now.

Q: What does a fraternity do for you?

A: It gives me a chance to be more social, 'cause I haven't in the past been a very social person. I, more or less, went to my room, did my schoolwork and that was it. I mean, now at Alpha, in a lot of the activities we do, I'm forced to have committee meetings and meeting with people that I have never been involved with. They also push you to be in different kind of clubs, and so they always support you and stuff like that. And just seeing—well actually most of them are a lot older than me, and seeing them getting jobs, graduating, and stuff like that, with the type of GPA [they get] they do graduate, that means a lot to me.

Q: Have you been involved in any of the activities in The President's Men program?

A: No, I'm just a recent member.

Q: Do you look forward to going out into the public school system and speaking to young students?

A: Yeah, last year we did that. We went to Booker T. Washington. And I was kind of nervous at first, but when we got up there, and some of the questions they asked me, I could really relate to it, because having friends that had just died from drugs, I mean, recently, on TV, and stuff like that, it really touched me. I feel like if I can help somebody out, studying and what not, so be it.

Q: What is the name of the organization that promoted that activity?

A: Men of Character.

Q: You also mentioned on the biographical form that you are vice president of the sophomore class. Would you speak a little bit about your involvement?

A: Well, we just came off of a successful week with the sophomore class. I, under the direction of KB, more or less, got some of the activities together as far as the gospel extravaganza we had, and things like that. It gives me a good chance, because I'm not one that likes to be seen. I just like to do the work behind the scenes.

Q: In that role, do you mostly do the work behind the scenes?

A: Yes. Not all of it, but a good percentage of it. I feel like, if you do it behind the scenes, the pressure is not looked upon as you. I mean, you can do it at your own moderate pace, and you don't have to be constantly nagged about when it is going to be done—you set your own pace.

Q: Your biographical sheet states that you are majoring in the field of business administration. Do you feel that you are a good organizer?

A: Yes.

Q: Are there any activities and organizations that you can identify as being important to your continued development?

A: Once again, the Alphas, because with this group of men, you have individuals from all walks of life. You have individuals, especially at this college, from the Virgin Islands, the Bahamas. You learn a lot about the culture. I eat with them, you know, you be with them, and stuff like that, and they're knowledgeable in all subjects; if I need something on law, I could speak to a certain individual, and stuff like that.

Q: What are the reasons why these activities and organizations are important to you?

A: I think, more or less, because in a sense it gives me the chance to grow, because I see life as one big, one big obstacle, and surrounded by lesser obstacles, and constantly, as I always—I always set life, even when I'm exercising, I set a limit where, let's say, I want to run a hundred yards, or what not. By the time I get to that finish line, that's like during the whole process you be tired, but to me, it's more like something is constantly pulling you down and that could be your career goal. If you complete it, you know you're to get—it's a challenge. You know, I just go out there and just say, "Well, I'm gonna run two miles if I can." If I don't stop, I know there's no doubt in my mind that I'll keep my goal.

Q: What is inside you that motivates you to succeed?

A: I just think, just do the best I can, because unlike some people, I don't look for a lot of people to commend me. I like to just do it myself. I work hard. It's a lot that I expect out of life, and it's a lot I intend to achieve out of life—and I don't feel like anything can stop me. Self—I think just more or less self-motivation. It gotta be from within.

Q: What passes through your thoughts when you have to make a decision?

A: How it would affect my mother, 'cause, I mean, she has done a lot for me, and I would hate to fail her, although I'm a person that initiates my motivation. I just always think of how would she look at it, or something like that.

Q: What would you say to young black men in the community? What message would you give to them?

A: That there is help out there, I mean, I hear a lot about it's no role model, but there are role models out there. That's all you have to do is go out and speak to individuals, because when people see that you're having a problem, I don't know a lot of people that will turn their head at you, because there are people that are out there that want to help you. You don't even have to go too far—it'll be the person next door, or whatnot. But you can get—whatever situation you're in now—you can always do better, no matter what.

Q: And what are your goals?

A: I plan to get a master's in business administration, and probably working in a bank as a banker, or something like that—have a nice family.

OBSERVER'S COMMENTS

After the taped interview, the following remarks ensued in conversation: Asked what he had learned about mixed cultures in his neighborhood, he responded that he was exposed to different styles of music, attitudes, needs;

- brother, thirteen years older, helped him regarding relationships, but in earlier years "hated" his brother, because he felt he was a bully;

- family did the most for him, tried to get him to be more social;

- respondent wanted to be alone with dog, "ran" dog near Joe Robbie Stadium; he "ran" to relax; tragedy occurred in his life when dog died, hit by car;

- sense of strong independence; would rather stay in dorm, even over holidays (last one to leave); feels that this is "mine"; when at home, feels he wants to leave, wants to be independent;

- success factor "mother" (housemaid), always buys him clothes; always talks to mother; never had a curfew, always knew when to come home; built-in sense of responsibility;

- saw father every two weeks, gave him a "little" money, here and there; never bothered him "not" seeing father;

- brother, thirteen years older, was someone to learn from (good and bad); learned from brother's mistakes;

- he also learned from his thirty-eight-year-old sister; she enjoys the finer things in life, such as movies, vacations;

- he feels that the "right" group of people is important; the long haul is better that the "quick" money;

- not happy with GPA 3.1; would like it to go up;

- he is a Compact Scholarship student; his life: books, library, school.

Description: very quiet, very conservative—
"WHATEVER BROTHER DOES, DOES OPPOSITE"

INTERVIEW 30

Q: Where were you born?

A: Homestead, Florida.

Q: Are you still living in Homestead?

A: Yes, I am.

Q: Who lived in your home with you as you were growing up?

A: My brother—my two older brothers, a younger sister, my mother, me and an older sister.

Q: Can you describe your home?

A: Basically, no money, a lot of hard work, closeness—that's about it.

Q: How many bedrooms did you have in your home?

A: Three.

Q: Did you have to share a bedroom with any of your siblings?

A: My two older brothers.

Q: Did you enjoy sharing a bedroom or was it a problem?

A: Yes, I enjoyed it—growing up with my two older brothers. They taught me things and sometimes I taught them things.

Q: Do you see anyone of them as a mentor?

A: Yes, I do, my older brother, C. Growing up, I was athletic, so he taught me how to wrestle and play football.

Q: How much older is he than you are?

A: About six years.

Q: Was he also your role model?

A: No, he wasn't. It was my mother.

Q: Why was your mother your role model?

A: I guess she always motivated me, never put me down, if I failed, she failed with me, and when I did something successful, she was always there, so I guess that's the reason she was my role model.

Q: Could you describe the neighborhood that you grew up in?

A: It was like a family; everyone knew each other; everyone helped out each other when they could. Sometimes, you had problems with landlords about cleaning up, typical things, but, basically, it was just more like a family.

Q: Did you have any peer group pressures in your neighborhood?

A: Yes, I guess that's in every neighborhood—it was there. You had the guys that would sell drugs, the guys that formed their own games, and you also had the guys that was athletic, so it was just. . . .

Q: How did you cope with that?

A: It wasn't a negative point; it was a positive point, because through peer pressure groups I seen, I can better myself and that's one reason I came to college, and I was able to cope with it.

Q: Did you always have the vision that you were going to go to college?

A: Yes, I did. One reason is because before I came to this college, I attended a junior college on a wrestling scholarship, and, basically, growing up, I was, I guess, "a best athletic," and I was decent—pretty decent.

Q: Were you friendly with the groups that were doing illegal things in the neighborhood?

A: Yes, I was, and today I still am, but them are the type of people I grew around all my life, them the type of people I'm accustomed to, that I can talk to, and I guess they know that I'm not with the selling drugs and gang banging, but they take me for me, not as part of a gang or selling drugs, and that's basically it.

Q: Primarily, were you involved in athletics?

A: Yes, I was. I was in football—"all-county defensive back" in my senior year, and, in wrestling, I was "all-county wrestler" in my senior year and also took second in the state of Florida, two years in a row—'90 and '91, so that's basically it.

Q: Did the younger boys look up to you?

A: Yes, they did. I have a lot of younger guys coming up to me, talking 'bout they liked my style in wrestling, and now they have learned my style and wrestling my style today, so, yeah, it's a lot of young guys that look up to me.

Q: Based on your grade-point average, would you say that you are a successful student, today?

A: Yes, yes, I will, because coming through high school, I wasn't really taught as much as I think I should have, and by coming to college, I have learned so much more, and I think that's one reason why I'm motivated, because I'm learning new things, and it's keeping me going.

Q: What factors do you identify as contributing to your success?

A: Thanks to having a daughter at a young age, and I guess my mother, by her being there and knowing that I can become someone; I think that really motivated me, that I have to do the right thing. I have two older brothers and a sister that wasn't quite successful, so I guess it's up to me, and so it's passed on down to me, so I know I have to do the right thing.

Q: How old were you when you had your daughter?

A: Eighteen.

Q: Do you take care of her at this time?

A: Yes, I do. [He spends as much time with her as his school schedule will allow.]

Q: Where does she live?

A: Miami Beach.

Q: What factors do you identify that could have been obstacles to your success?

A: I guess I could have easily turned to the street life, because the life I grew up with, I had to learn the streets at an early age, so I guess the streets could have been one obstacle that could have shot at my success, but I have a strong mind, and I have a will to succeed, so I guess that's one reason I didn't turn to the streets.

Q: What course of action did you take to overcome obstacles that you encountered, for example, the "streets"?

A: Basically, sports; I guess sports was the way that occupied my time and that really turned me away from the streets, and coaches that was dedicated to me and what I was doing, so I guess that's one way I overcame the obstacle of turning to the streets.

Q: Were any of your coaches your role models?

A: No, I think my brother really was my role model, because coming up, my brother was also, as I seen it, this excellent wrestler, and, in a way, I wanted to be the type of wrestler he was, so I guess no coaches, he was my older brother.

Q: In speaking about major influences in your life, could you speak about the influence of your family ?

A: My family was always there, you know, and right today they are still standing behind me 100 percent. I guess growing up with a single parent, mother paralyzed, income under $10,000, you had to become bonded as one, and I guess right today, we as one, we love each other, so I guess that's the role that they played in my life.

Q: Did she become ill after you were born?

A: Yes, she did.

Q: What happened?

A: My mother was shot, accidentally shot in the back, by her ex-husband and was paralyzed from the hips up.

Q: How did that affect you?

A: I think my mom has shown me being paralyzed is that the strong can survive, and my mom was so strong that she was able to take care of five kids with an income of lower than $10,000, and gave us a life that, to me, was exciting, so that's the reason I'm joining special education.

Q: On your biographical sheet, you state that you are majoring in special education. What reasons can you give for majoring in special education?

A: To influence kids that it's a life after that—it's a life even if you are handicapped, paralyzed, whatever, so it's a life after that, and you can have a successful life.

Q: Could you proceed with the major influences in your life? Do you recount any teachers who were influential?

A: Yes, I had a assistant coach while coming up. He was also my shop teacher, and he gave me a part-time job—to keep away from the streets. He gave me books to read. He took me to the national tournament, so I guess he was an influence.

Q: And your peers?

A: I would have to say again, my peers would be my friends. They was there. I was an influence to everyone, a sports activity match, anything, I did good in school, they congratulated me on, so I guess friends, basically.

Q: Previously you mentioned that some of your peers were involved in illegal activities. What would you say would be the percentage of your peer group that was involved in illegal activities—friends that you grew up with in the same area?

A: I'd probably say about 70 percent.

Q: Did they outgrow it?

A: No.

Q: Why don't you think they outgrew it?

A: I basically think they was forced into that life. My friends that have sometimes, six and seven members in their family, and they seen that way to support they family. Some of them at the time was evicted, and they know that to survive they was either gonna have to turn to the streets or to a job that was, at the time, paying $4.35 per hour, what will be no help at all, so I think that's one way they turned to the streets, and I don't see it as a downfall, I just see it as a way of surviving.

Q: And what were the percentages that were caught and put in jail?

A: About 30 percent.

Q: Do you think that young people, dealing in illegal activities, have any future?

A: Definitely not, because at this point, they looking at short term, not long term, so I guess in another twenty to thirty years, they'll be lost in that cycle, that coming from the ghetto, that mostly majority of the kids is caught up in, so I guess they will probably raise kids in that same cycle, and, I guess, life goes on and on.

Q: Did you ever see yourself being "pulled down" in that way?

A: Yes, plenty of times. One time my mom was evicted and by learning the streets at a early age, I knew that I can get out there and survive, so at certain times, I wanted to, but through the influence of my mom and brothers, I actually stayed away from it, but it's been plenty of times where I wanted to turn to the streets to survive.

Q: To continue, could you speak about the influence of athletics in your life?

A: Through my brother I learned sports at a early age. By the age of seven, I was wrestling in the national tournaments. By the time I was in junior high, I was considered one of the best wrestlers in the nation in my age group. By the time I was in senior high, athletics gave to me a sense of going to college. I knew that was the only way I was gonna get out of the ghetto, so that's how athletics helped me out, you know what I'm saying, a way to get out of the ghetto, a way to become someone and just to give back. That's the way athletics helped me.

Q: Was the church an influence?

A: I came up in a Baptist church, but at the present time, I have no religion. I'm seeking for that religion. I'm trying to find my own religion.

Q: And role models that you can think of—other than the ones you mentioned—your mother, your brother, your coach, any role models in society?

A: I would have to say Les Brown. I think how he was stereotyped as illiterate coming up, and became probably one of the most successful black motivational speakers in the world, and I think Les Brown is probably one of my motivaters. [Les Brown grew up in Liberty City.]

Q: What activities and organizations can you identify as being important to your continuing development?

A: I would have to say being around kids; I think this was something I wanted to do—I wanted to give back. I feel that coming up the way I did wasn't just negative, it was also positive. I think if I can give back at least just to one person, I'll feel better.

Q: What can you as a successful college student at a historically black college recommend or advise young black males?

A: I would have to say give life a chance, further the education, because education is knowledge, and knowledge is how you become successful, and I think that everyone has to look at students that's not going to college and are in two different perspectives—I think that the ones that can't make a living right now, and the one's that's on the streets is hard—once you're in it, it's hard to turn away, so what I leave with them is that I'm not booting nothing they do, it's just that right now I have to try to survive 'cause I feel that they in a lost society and that's one way they're trying to survive, so I just, you know what I'm saying, hope that they are safe and decide one day to do the right thing.

Q: And the right thing would be?

A: Further their education, change their cycle that their family been going through for years and years, and that's something I want to do.

Q: What is inside you that motivates you to succeed?

A: I guess the conditions that I was brought up in, my mother, that cycle that my family, again, had been going through, generation after generation, I think that's what's making me succeed.

Q: Out of the five young people in your family, what other children have taken the same positive route that you have taken?

A: My older brother have, but things haven't really been too successful for him, so, I guess, I would really say none, just me at this present time.

Q: What passes through your thoughts when you have to make a decision?

A: Oh, is it gonna be the right decision, am I gonna fall in that cycle of turning to the streets, if I'm not successful, where will I end up, the fear of failing, I guess these are the kind thoughts I go through when making decisions.

Q: Did you miss not having a father in your home when you were growing up?

A: Yes, I did. In a way, I had my father there, but not as a perspective as taking care of me, or being there for me, it was just some weekends, we wasn't able to develop a relationship, because he had a family outside of our family, so, I guess, in a way, I did, because I was this curious young boy coming up, so I feel that I needed a father around. I was a terrific athlete, and, I guess, in a way, my brother played that daddy role, because he was always there for me, every wrestling match, he was there, every football game, so, basically, I wish I did have a father, but my brother played that role, and I have to live with it.

Q: Is that why you place a major emphasis on being with your daughter?

A: Definitely yes, I do. I guess I want to grow up, and let my daughter know I was a father, that I was always here, that my daddy loves me, that I can be able to take care of her financially, and one day I will be able to do it with no problem, always there for her, more time, and I guess, basically, just play my role—I just really want to be a father.

OBSERVER'S COMMENTS

Description of respondent:

- 5 feet 9 inches, 172 pounds;

- white, long-sleeved sweater, black jeans;

- from respondent's words: "fun-loving personality"; outspoken, sometimes, with friends; reserved, observant, "sees how he can relate"; mom has survived, "Where there is a will, there is a way";

- mom now brings up sister's five children; mother has legal custody of children; respondent did learn "positive" things from the street; he used examples of bad situations to steer his own survival: he went in the "opposite direction"; he saw "young people taken to jail";

- he wants to break cycle of stagnation, deprived ghetto life for his family; wants to own his own home;

- he wants "to give a lot back to the community, because he received a lot from the community";

- various programs that helped him: sports activities, attended speeches, went to parks, anything that kept him away from the streets;

- project upbringing: did everything in the projects, everybody took care of each other;

- he said that those who lived in the project called it "Drive U Nuts";—he was born in the project, still lives there, refers to it as "a prison."

AWARDS

- Junior High School: B Honor Roll; 2 times county champ in wrestling

- Senior High School: 2 times state runner-up, all-county wrestling; all-county in football, 1991; Wrestler of the Year, 1991

- College: Academic Compact Scholarship; Honor Roll; President's Men

INTERVIEW 31

Q: Who lived in your home with you as you were growing up?

A: My mother and my brothers were the only individuals with myself in my household when I was growing up.

Q: How many children were in the family?

A: Seven children were in the family.

Q: How many girls and how many boys?

A: Seven boys, no girls.

Q: Can you describe the home you grew up in—the physical aspects of it?

A: My home that I grew up in was extremely clean, although we didn't have quite a bit of material things, but very clean, very organized, so to speak, but not a lot of materialistic things; we had the basic necessities, but not a lot of Persian rugs and things of that nature.

Q: How many bedrooms were in your home?

A: We had approximately, because it was several different places that I lived—the minimum of at least three bedrooms, but most of my brothers—I'm the youngest, my other brothers are about eight years older than I am—most of them were out of the house when I was growing up, so we had about three bedrooms, and I shared a bedroom with someone else, and I think my other brothers had their own bedroom—something like that.

Q: Can you describe the neighborhood you grew up in?

A: Probably the most memorable part of my growing up would be my high school—and the neighborhood I grew up was equivalent to what we called the "projects," a lot of apartment buildings in one area; I would say not a lot of opportunities, not a lot of activities going on, just mostly predominantly low income, low housing.

Q: Can you describe the feelings inside your home?

A: My home was always filled with a lot of love, and attention, and although we were in environments that really wasn't conducive of that, it was always a lot of love, a lot of feelings—we're not going to be in this situation all our lives, so it was a lot of love always and lot of hope in my home.

Q: Based on your grade-point average, would you say that you are a successful student?

A: Well, personally, I don't think a GPA by itself measures success, but as far as my own personal GPA and my situation that I come from, I think I'm a success, just to be able to be to the level that I am, first of all—but as far as my GPA, I don't necessarily think that is a true barometer of success for myself, as well as many other people. But to answer your question, I guess, I would be successful, not because of my GPA, but because of the obstacles that I overcame to obtain a GPA.

Q: What are some of those obstacles?

A: Single-parent home—not really having the best or getting the average amount of certain things that most kids had—I mean not just the level of toys, or the level of cars, but more like certain types of clothing that in high school is sort of difficult, 'cause most kids, you know, are judged in accordance to their dress code, and at the same time, I didn't have other people that went on to have high levels of education, so in a sense, I really didn't have anyone to say, "Well, this is what you need to do." I had people telling me to stay out of trouble, and walk the right road, but not necessarily saying, "Well, you need to make sure you study for your SAT, so you can get admittance to college," or that type of direction; those are the disadvantages.

Q: How would you define the word success?
A: Success, to me, is probably different than what it is to many other people. Success for one man may be different than it is for another man. Success is overcoming the obstacles that you'll maybe face. Some people's obstacles may be drug abuse, or drug addiction. Some other people's may be passing a calculus course. To me, first of all, it begins with knowing one's self. I think once you know yourself, you're automatically successful, because that is the beginning of really everything—self-esteem, self-confidence, every-thing—self-gratitude starts with, or confidence starts with, all those different things. It helps those things develop. So, to me, success is knowing self—that's what I define as success.
Q: What factors do you identify as contributing to your success?
A: Definitely, my mother's belt, my mother's abilities, and ways of making sure that I never lost faith of God, make sure that I was a man first, was able to go out and make my own money, work and earn an honest living; my mother and my brothers would make sure that I stayed out of trouble, because if I didn't, my mother would beat, as well as them—so those—God, my mother, my brothers and family were the contributing factors to whatever I will be, or whatever I am now.
Q: Did your father ever live in the home with you?
A: When I was young, my mother left my father when I was about three or four, but I used to live with my father every summer for about four years during my junior high school/elementary range, but prior to my birth, they used to live together, but after my birth, shortly after that, they didn't live together.
Q: Has your father contributed to your success?
A: Yes, in a different fashion than the others. He contributed more as a disciplinarian. He was a person that was a no-nonsense type of person, and he taught me that I wasn't special. I wasn't someone that was just gonna walk into somebody's office, or interview, and was just gonna take something, because I was who I am. He taught me that I had to work hard for everything I had, or would like to have, and to know that the only way that I can achieve those goals is through hard work and dedication.
Q: You mentioned obstacles previously. What course of action did you take to overcome the obstacles that you encountered?
A: Recently, if you want to mention obstacles, and things that I have done—first of all, finding self, knowing that I can do anything I want to do if I put my mind to it. That was the major problem with me when I was younger, and when I was in junior high school, and high school, because I didn't really have knowledge of self, so the obstacles, the biggest obstacle for myself was knowing who I am, and my abilities are just as equivalent as the next person and can be even greater if I apply myself.
Q: On your biographical sheet, you state that you are an airway computer science major?
A: Yes, I am.
Q: Why did you decide on that major?
A: First of all, throughout high school, I've always been an analytical person. Mathematics has always been a very interesting field for me, and I felt that computer science is the future; it's today and it's also the future, and aviation is definitely part of the future. Growing up in the environment that I grew up in, I realized that I couldn't just go to college to just go to college, I had to go to college and study something that is a part of the future, so I decided airway computer science, because I feel I have the attitude, as well as the aptitude, to obtain those goals.
Q: What were the major influences in your life other than your family?

A: Other than my family, definitely God. I was brought up to, number one, keep faith in God, but to be honest with you, I really never had a lot of outside elements affecting me outside of my family, because I was the youngest, and I stayed pretty much within my family—the walls of my own household—but, I had people that I looked up to like Martin Luther King, Malcolm X, but to be honest with you, until recently, I really never knew the significance of them, or the attributes that they even had.

Q: Were any of your teachers influential in your life?

A: Present-day teachers, yes, but in the manner of challenging me, in the manner of not allowing me to settle for less than I can accomplish, when they know I can get an A in the course—no one particular person that stood out—it's been a combination of just a lot of people that have contributed, but no one person any greater than the other. It's just me realizing, living in society that really, many times, people will help you without necessarily trying to help you, you know; I've had a lot of negative forms of help—getting fired from a job, a person who helped me one time, to realize certain things—so I never had a lot of individual people, but it's just a group of people in situations, and circumstances, that helped me.

Q: For instance, getting fired from a job, how did that help you?

A: The way I lost the job was I realized certain things. I realized that life, everything in life, does not follow the pattern that I was brought up to think—that everyone was going to respect everyone's ability to do certain things, and what's yours is yours, and what's theirs is theirs, and I was in a situation where I was unjustly accused of certain things, and that helped me mature and realize that those things are going to happen. And when you don't realize that—regardless of how good you are, how hard you work—that negative things are going to happen to you, anyway. I mean, I was never prepared for it, and losing a job prepared me for, regardless of how well I do academically, I'm still at the mercy of those that I have to go see for a job, so that helps me to want to become my own owner. I want to be an entrepreneur. I want to own my own business, and that way I can't fire myself.

Q: Were your peers an influence in your life?

A: Yes, and in the same fashion, a negative fashion. I have about seven friends that are in jail. I have one that has a life sentence. I have several others that are probably going to be in jail for the rest of their lives, so it's in a negative fashion to see—you see, I saw enough of the other side to realize that something else has to be better than that. I have a friend named OCS; I have a friend named DRS; DH—these are people that were good people—I saw good people that just went the wrong way, so my friends, yes, they helped me, but in doing negative things, helped me to realize that that's not the way to go.

Q: What courses of action did you take that led you in another direction?

A: My mother was the primary source, and I guess, the fortune in the fact that God was looking over me, because I didn't do anything special, any different than anybody else, but I just feel like now that I've analyzed my life, it seems as though someone was looking out for me. My mother is very religious. She does a lot of praying for me, even now. So, she kept me mentally on the right track, although when you are adolescent, sometimes you can know what's right and still do wrong. So, the main things I did was just try to live and do the right things, and I had a good righteous heart and I think "luck"; I guess you can say "luck"; I guess you can say "fate" brought me to where I'm at now, because I didn't really do anything special. I don't want to make myself out a hero. I didn't do anything special than my friends did. I think they probably were in worse situations; their family members were on drugs. I had strong family support, so I guess that would be the strong family support that kept me away from it.

Q: Were athletics an influence in your life?

A: Yes, not as much as most people, but to a certain degree when I was in high school. That was the only thing that I had going for me. I didn't really think on the level of education. I was on the basketball team and just like, I guess, every other young kid in the inner city, I wanted to be just like Julius Irving and Larry Bird, so that was something probably greater than my education, and greater than going to college. That was something that try to push me through high school, the fact that I could go to college to play basketball, then hopefully, go to the next level, so, yeah, athletics helped a great deal.

Q: Who are your role models?

A: My mother. I guess my mother would have to be the one and only. My brothers contributed a lot. I respect a lot of them, but as far as one individual, I really can't—my mother and my father contributed a lot—but my mother, I respect her the most because she, as a woman, taught me how to be a man, and I'd respect any person that can do that, so my mother is my role model.

Q: How did she teach you "to be a man"?

A: First of all, I think the greatest thing she taught me, and it sticks with me now, is the fact of always trying to be independent of anything—don't be dependent upon the government, don't be dependent on any form of systems, whether it is welfare system, or whatever, but to be able and have the conscience of mind to go out and make your own money; be able to live within your own means, so that one day you can have more than you have today—so my mother, she is a person, I guess, if she has lot of money, she probably would be a rich person 'cause she can handle money well, it's just that she's never ran across quite a bit—so my mother.

Q: Did the church influence your life? Did you attend church when you were young?

A: In my earlier days, we lived in the church for the most part. When we got older, my mother was a person that was always about letting you decide and letting you be the person that chose your faith in life. She would guide you in the right direction, but as far as religion is concerned, she doesn't feel that that's something that—as far as what form of religion or what type, or if you want to be a Baptist, or you want to be a Protestant, or if you want to be a Muslim, a Catholic or whatever—she didn't feel as though that was something that she had to tell us, "Well, this is what you're gonna do"; so when we were younger, she taught us the right way to go; now, I don't go as much, and it's not due to the fact that I don't have strong faith, it's just the fact that college has kind of changed me to a certain degree, that a lot of my priorities have gone from spiritual to economics, or educational, but right now, I don't attend church regularly.

Q: What activities and organizations can you identify as being important to your continuing development?

A: I would have to say, that's a good question; right now, I think the activities that will probably contribute to most of my continuing development will be—I don't know if it's a organization, but what helps me the most now— to help other people that are younger than myself, that I feel don't see some of the things I see. I know that's maybe not organization, but it's an activity. Like many freshman now that not only don't see the proper way of doing things, as far as educationally, but as far as mentally and spiritually, as well. Those things help me, in turn, you know how when you help someone do math—in a sense, it helps you, too, because you're going over it, and you're understanding it a little better than you probably did before, so when I go over certain things with, like a freshman guy that I know named IC, it helps me to develop myself, because not only am I going to explain it to him, I'm explaining it to myself—unless I'm going to talk to myself out loud, that's something I can't do—so those activities helped me to develop, continue to develop.

Q: What are the reasons why these activities are important?

A: Because, to me, I feel that if they're important, because if I would have been told, or seen, some of the things I'm telling other people now, I could have made a change in my life a lot sooner, not that I was living terrible, but until I found myself, and knew who I was, and had self-confidence, I wasn't able to go to that next level, because I was always afraid; I didn't feel—in certain societies, people divide black and white, and the society I was in, it was divided—but once I had self-confidence, I crossed the line, and I dared anyone to tell me that I didn't belong there, because I knew I did—academically, athletically, in any form, I felt that I was equivalent to anyone educationally, so I forgot the question itself but. . . .

Q: The reasons of activities being important. . . .

A: . . . Yeah, it's been important to me, because it shows me that although I didn't get it exactly when I deserved it, I received it, and it's my duty to continue the cycle, and if I can help one person to understand something that I see—I get a lot of self-gratification, self-fulfillment out of that.

Q: And organizations?

A: I've never really been a part of, I've always been a shy person until recently. I've never been a member of the NAACP, or any form of fraternity; The President's Men is one organization that I've been a part of, but at the same time, in my development, it's more to it as far as to help other people, although, I haven't really had the opportunity to help other people yet, but as far as organization, I don't really have any organization; it's more of an activity that I, independently, do on my own, or whenever I get the opportunity. You might see me just talking to someone I don't even know, because it's something that is meaningful to me, because I sort of lived through a certain life that some people may say it's really not bad, but if that's not bad, then I feel that the standards that we're living in now are terrible, because I saw a lot of negativity, and for me, to be where I'm at now, after seeing and being faced with a lot of different situations, it's sort of, it's almost unbelievable. I shouldn't even be here, really, to be honest with you.

Q: Could you give an example of a negative situation that you can recall?

A: There's quite a few, but I guess I've been in situations where I've never been a person that initiated, or just really got enjoyment out of negative situations, but I've been a part of a lot of negative situations, as far as, like I've had friends, many friends of mine, we were just hanging out, and sometimes we would just be walking—nothing to do, just nothing to do—it'll be either summer—and just nothing to do—one friend would go around . . . robbing. Those situations, I didn't experience a lot, but I experienced enough to be able to understand, and realize, that that's not the way of life that I want to live, that's not the style. I guess probably the most, the worse situation, I would say, would be when I was home; all of my friends lived in the projects. But once I graduated, my mother moved into a brand-new home, and people thought that we were better than those in the projects, but we didn't have much, but a lot of people didn't realize that it wasn't that much to live in a house. My mother got a house built, and I lived next to, let's say, about ten blocks from the projects, and then all of my friends were in the projects, so I used to go in the projects and hang with my friends. Most of those sold drugs. Most of my friends sold drugs, so it wasn't an uncomfortable feeling for me or abnormal for me to see them doing it, as we spoke with each other. . . . [Yet], I don't think you have to see [repeated frightening incidents] if you're a righteous person to realize that's not right, that's not the way to live.

Q: Would you know the statistics on the number of friends that you have that would be involved in those kinds of activities?

A: My early childhood, I would say probably about 80 percent of the friends that I had were involved in—I mean, maybe not to that extent, but juvenile offenses. In my high school years, it sort of decreased, because I don't know, I guess that maybe it was the company I was around. I guess after my mother moved into the house, and we were really in an integrated community, and everyone had homes, and everyone pretty much stayed to themselves, most of my friends—I didn't have many friends—I guess, the number probably then would be about 10 percent, so I guess the community, and the environment that I was in had a lot to do with it.

Q: When you were in that project environment, did you envision a way out?

A: Definitely not. I did not see a road, a path, or whatever word you would like to use. I didn't see anything. The only thing I saw was—it was more important for me to stay out of trouble, than it was for me to worry about would it be a better day. For instance, I mean, a person in that environment, probably, if he graduated from high school, and went to the army, he was an enormous success, so I didn't see myself to where I'm at now. I didn't see myself in a negative situation, either because of the fact that no one in my family, even my brothers that was older, none of them had negative images, because all of them got their education, but it's just that I didn't see it on the level of college, or on the level of a master's or Ph.D. I just recently learned what that was, so I'm not gonna say that it was terrible, but it wasn't good, it wasn't good. I didn't see the level of making $20,000 a year. If I'd have been able to make that, that would have been like a dream, you know; whereas now, if someone offered me a job for that, it would probably be like an insult.

Q: How old are you now?

A: I'm twenty-five years now. I started school, I came to this college when I was twenty-one, because of the fact that for one, I didn't know much about college. I thought you had to have, I thought it was only for people that had money, and I used to tutor friends of mine that went to college when I was in high school, but they had family members that went to college, also, and their family had more financial means than my family did, so I thought it was just an economic type of thing, so I went to a trade school for two years, and then, basically, I was just working. I've worked since I was fifteen. . . . I've been working since, let's see, about ten years, so that's the positive thing that kept me out of trouble, because I've worked and had my own money, so when my friends went out and stole, I didn't have to do that. My mother and father didn't give it to me, but I had my own. In high school I was making $100 a week, which was good at that time.

Q: Why do you think your friends stole?

A: Most of the friends that I grew up with had terrible family support, terrible. One friend of mine, I don't want to use any explicit words, but his mother was a lesbian, I hope I can say that, and her lover used to lived with them. His sisters—he had two sisters— resorted to prostitution, and his other sisters are also lesbians; his brothers, they stayed in jail; I think, they probably are still in jail now, so him and myself, we were both the same age, but he didn't have the same things I had. I had brothers that were on the basketball team; I had brothers that were working; I had brothers that the community admired, because they weren't in trouble. So, him and I, I don't think he even had a chance. I think right now he's on drugs, but those are some of the major differences in my household than my friend's household. The guy didn't even have a chance, because one of his sisters passed away. She got murdered, and they threw her body somewhere— this was when I was living in the projects—threw her body somewhere in some dumpster by their house. Growing up in that kind of environment, I don't see how he could have made anything of himself, and then again, like I said, he did pretty good, because I think he got to the eleventh grade. That was considered good, because he didn't result to selling drugs until later—selling drugs is not good, but under the situation he was in, I was surprised that it took him that long—terrible situation, but as I mentioned before, I never was the type of person that could do that. I had too much—my brothers and my mother; I was the youngest of seven brothers, and the brother next to me is like five years older, so I was a lot smaller than everybody else, so I never tried to challenge my brothers. I had one brother that kinda stayed a little bit in trouble, but he, for some reason, if he saw me trying to get in trouble, he was just like he was a monk, and whenever he came to me, I had to be purified. I had to go wash my hands, and everything I had to correct, so I applaud him for that.

Q: Do you think he knew the difference between right and wrong.

A: Yes, he did. Even though he still did a lot of negative things, nothing to compare to anything that I mentioned about anyone else, you know; he would probably skip school, which is negative; he'd get in fights at school, but it was nothing to the point that he was expelled, or he was selling drugs, or he robbed anyone—nothing to that effect.

Q: Do you think your friends knew the difference between right and wrong?

A: Yes, all of my friends. As a matter of fact, I have a friend now that's in jail someplace; I'm writing him now, and he's saying the same thing he said before. He knows the difference between right and wrong; it's just the fact that he didn't see where doing right was going to benefit him. He felt that if "wrong" was going to benefit him, then that's what he would do, and, I think, that was due to the fact that he didn't see any way to the future. He didn't see any positive things down the road, so he was living for the day, and if he can have twenty dollars today, then he would try to get twenty dollar by any means necessary.

Q: Are you speaking about a friend in a time frame of fifteen years ago? Is it that long ago?

A: Yes.

Q: What do you think are the major problems today? In the news every day, we see, hear, and read about an inordinate amount of violence. According to your perceptions, is it any different from fifteen years ago, and, if so, what caused that change?

A: Yes, the type of violence has changed dramatically from the last fifteen years. Primarily, I feel, due to crack cocaine has contributed a major portion, because of the type of drug it is. It is a very addictive drug that literally takes the mind away from the person and eliminates what any form of morals and ethics that really is the backbone of the family structure; a person of fifteen years ago may have had children, may have been on drugs, may have been on marijuana, or whatever, but marijuana doesn't have the same effect—it doesn't necessarily change your ethics and morals, and it's not something that will necessarily make you feel, or desire, to kill someone or take from someone. I think once the nation was exposed to crack cocaine, it just automatically took the family structure, and just broke it in half, because we had mothers who were already in a situation that they were single-parent mothers and were beginning to neglect children because of the need for the drug. Then we have a generation of children growing up with no guidance, no real form of discipline, and no hope, really, and then once you have a situation like that, then you have a lot of teenage violence, you have a lot of escalating teenage drop-out rate, an escalating number of teenage pregnancies, and abortion levels are rising, because the morals of the country, and the people are changing with the family structure. Most of my morals have been set within me, within my family structure. Now, had I not have had those set in place, I definitely wouldn't be where I'm at, nor the person that I am, so I think crack cocaine took a generation of people away, and the part of the people that survived, don't have the same form of morals, and ethics that the previous generations had.

Q: Do you think crack cocaine is used more by young blacks than young whites?

A: I would say maybe "used," maybe "not so much"; I would say perhaps some young blacks have something—some way or the other—they have crack cocaine, whether they are using it, or selling it—to me, it's the same. I would say so, yes. If we were to say like pure cocaine, that's something different, but crack cocaine, I would say the young African American would probably be more involved in that, because selling it is a quick and profitable business, and using it is a quick high, so if you're in a society, or you're in a situation, and your race, or your family, don't have the financial means to be part of the elite, nor do you have the educational background to envision a future, I would feel that some young African Americans are either dealing, using, selling, or whatever, manufacturing crack cocaine, yes.

Q: Why don't they go out and get a job?

A: Because of what I mentioned earlier—when you don't have the family structure, and the role, and the goals and objectives of life set in your mind from an early age, you don't envision working at a job for enough years to move to a management level, or assistant manager, and maybe one day, a person that is a CEO or something; you don't envision that, because one person, who doesn't have any thoughts or any views of the future is only going to live for now, so getting a job, unless you're getting a respectable job, and, then, at the same time, like I said, we don't have people that are being brought up where working is what is considered what you should do. I know many people that are young and healthy that don't want to work; money in this society tells you what class you're in—if you have money you can be in a middle class or high class—if you don't have, then you're in a low class. Working seems like a good way of just eliminating a lot of the situation, but we have a society in which people grew up with no morals, with low morals, or no morals and ethics, and working was really not necessarily the only way of making money. People were making greater amounts of money selling drugs than people that had college degrees.

Q: Do you know of any solutions to this problem in our society?

A: My opinion is there's no one single solution. Everything has to be a societal type of thing, but I think, certain things could help it, maybe not eliminate it completely, but I know there is a certain level that we just can't take back. Once you put money in the telephone, you just can't get it back, so a certain part of our society, I'm not gonna say are lost forever, but the most important elements of a child, raising people to adulthood, are certain stages of childhood. The young generation can't take the dysfunctional family that they have, but I think some solutions would be, and I don't necessarily feel that they are even governmental type of things, but if I would want to throw in a governmental type of thing, I would feel that if we could do something, first of all, to eliminate the manufacturing of all these illegal drugs that we have, and some people may not feel that that's important, but I feel that the crack cocaine started it—to get to the point that it is now. The illegal drugs, as far as the crack cocaine, and then we have the gun manufacturers, we could talk all day and people say, "Why are young kids having guns?" but they are not getting them from anywhere—I think, in this country, the business of this country has always been business, so a lot of times we know something is hurting us, but if it's making us money, then we may not necessarily do anything about it, but as far as guns, and crime, and young people, I think drugs and guns are the biggest two weapons, although it starts with the person making the decision to pull the trigger, and the person has to make the decision to smoke the drugs. I don't think there's any form of legislation you can use to say where you have to raise your kids the right way, but I think with the elimination of certain types of drugs like crack cocaine, and laws against the easy availability of handguns, will turn threatening situations into less harmful situations—ending up in a fistfight or wrestling instead of a shootout, or a person putting a child in the trash. We don't have enough social reform in this country. It's more of a financial reform, but the social reform is really what's making the financial reform difficult to obtain.

Q: What can you as a successful student at a historically black college recommend or advise young black males?

A: First of all, what I can advise the young African Americans, it would be first to—it's difficult to instill certain things within yourself, because we're in a society sometimes that we don't always have—our leaders are not always the best qualified for the position, but I feel, as an individual—to try to find self, and what I mean by find self is to be able to have self-satisfaction in the fact that who you are, regardless if whether you're from the projects, or whether you're from a small town, just be able to be happy and content with the fact that you are a person that is a child of God, and you are here for a reason, and, then to obtain success through that. In my opinion, success is knowing self, so once you get to the point, and you know yourself, and you accept the fact that you can accomplish anything you would like to if you put your mind to it. I know that sounds kinda out of the question to many people that may be inner city, because if a person would have told me that, I would not have believed that. But my advice would be to, first of all, find yourself in society regardless of what someone else is doing and how much money somebody else is making. You have to find yourself, because conformity is the easiest thing to do. We can all conform to the norm, but until you come out of conformity, and you don't conform to what's normal, you're going to be a part of the negativity that's in the society, because society is negative right now. It's gonna take those who are away from that, and you gotta be outside the house to look at the house from the outside, so when you're inside the house, things seem differently, so if you find yourself as an individual and how you fit into society, and then, I think, that's the beginning—I can't say, well, listen to this person, or listen to that person, because everyone is not going to tell you the right thing. Every part of society is not going to work out, and even the government is not gonna always do what's best for its people, but if you know yourself first, and look at yourself outside of society and find a place for yourself, and, then, that is the beginning of it in my opinion.

Q: What is inside you that motivates you to succeed?

A: The main things that's inside of me to motivate me to succeed is the fact that when I was in Tampa, and I was working, and I was a young, ambitious, bright, young man, black or white, I was always told that I couldn't achieve. I was always told that—I was treated as though certain things were not for me, and I always told people before, what made me do something, if you want me to do something, tell me I can't do it, and then I'll do it, so that motivated me the most when I was in Tampa. I used to train employees that came in and out, but yet those same employees would move above me, myself, and it wasn't because of my lack of education, because I've always been pretty swift, in my opinion; I mean, maybe I didn't fit into certain cultures but, at the same time, I knew—you put something in front of me, and I could read it, and I could comprehend it just as well as the next person, so a person telling me that I can't, I couldn't do it, helped me to do it, and the reason why I came to this college is because members at my job in Tampa told me that I couldn't handle college, told me that that's not for me—and that's what motivated me.

Q: Why do you think they said that to you?

A: My opinion, it only had to be due to the fact that the society that they were in said that certain people couldn't do a certain thing other people could do—black people couldn't do certain things and white people could, because it couldn't be because of what I showed them, because I've always showed them, and I have always had a level; I displayed a level of excellence. I trained more people, I never had anything negative in any form, no type of reprimand, nothing negative, as far as my work and performance, so it only had to be that certain things in certain societies, you know, there was only a certain limit you were supposed to reach, and I'm not necessarily going to fault them—that society as a whole, but they felt that, they said, "Well, how much money do you have," I don't have any money. "How are you going to go to college with no money?" And society made them feel as though certain things had to be done—you had to have a certain amount of money, you had to have a certain amount of—if you were black—you had to be the kind of person that would almost like disenfranchise himself from his race, and I wasn't that type of person, so I guess for that reason, they felt that I wasn't gonna make it, 'cause they didn't know what school I was going to; but, I guess, they thought that I would go to a university, and that I wouldn't integrate with society, but I'm a very easy person to get along with, but I guess that their conformity to how society was in [my hometown] during that time, contributed to them feeling that I wouldn't make it, because my job performance was always excellent.

Q: What passes through your thoughts when you have to make a decision?

A: Most of the time my future experiences, my past experiences—every time I have to make any type of career decision, or any type of life-lasting decision, I think about what I've been through, and sometimes I get stressed out when I have a test, but then I realize what all I've been through—taking a test is really like a cakewalk—from experiencing fighting another neighborhood, because they came to our neighborhood—so my past experiences come to mind when I make any decision, and I think about a lot of the things I learned in the last years fifteen years, so those are the things, my past experiences come to my mind, before I make a decision, or when I make a decision.

Q: Were there gangs in your neighborhood?

A: No, there were not gangs, but they were like territorial type of things. You couldn't go to a certain neighborhood, if they knew you was from there, because I guess you just couldn't be there. It's a free country, you know, public land, but you just couldn't be there, because you didn't live there, so it wasn't really gangs, but it was the form of separation, segregation among the segregated.

Q: Would you like to add anything else to the interview?

A: Well, I would like to say first of all that I appreciate you allowing me to express some of my most personal things that I experienced in my past and in my life, and hopefully, that with this survey, or this interview, we can make—yourself and myself—we can make a positive difference in society. I mean, to me, it's kinda difficult to see it being done overnight, but to know that there are people like yourself that are trying, and whether it's for a paper or not, I just hope that we can make something positive happen with this situation.

OBSERVER'S COMMENTS

Respondent:
- is serious minded, focused, stays on track;
- is intellectual, insightful;
- believes that if he had a father in home, father would have helped him "get into football, helped in confidence at an earlier age";
- didn't join organizations, because of a lack of confidence;
- now can see himself in graduate school;
- worked an average of forty hours a week while in college until this semester;
- quit work this semester to get average up;
- is presently taking nineteen credit hours.

INTERVIEW 33

Q: Who lived in your home with you as you were growing up?

A: Well, it was me, my mother and my grandmother.

Q: Can you describe the home you grew up in?

A: It was a lot of discipline and most of the time when I was growing up my mom was in college, and my grandmother really kinda raised me and was like the father figure to me, so it was okay, but, even though there was no male in the home, I still felt that they did a good job in bringing me up because they kept me active in a lot of things to keep me busy. I think they did a pretty good job.

Q: What neighborhood in Miami did you grow up in?

A: It's a combination of two. The one that I spent the most time in was Opa-Locka, over by Joe Robbie Stadium, on the west side of 27th Avenue, over in that area, that's where I spent most of my time growing up.

Q: Could you describe that neighborhood?

A: Well, it's the type of neighborhood that where mostly everybody knew everybody and that was good in a way because everybody looked out for everyone and everything like that, but you did have those who were doing bad things like trying to break into people's homes and stuff like that, but since it was a close-knit neighborhood, everyone looked out for each other, and all the kids knew each other, we played together and everything like that. It was a pretty good environment I grew up in.

Q: What is your definition of success?

A: Well, the first thing that comes to mind is being financially stable and, but, there's a lot of things that comes along with that. I feel that being comfortable, healthy, being in a job that you enjoy doing and not living from paycheck to paycheck but living comfortably, that's what I see success as being.

Q: Based on your present grade-point average would you say that you are a successful student?

A: Well, it's mediocre. It could be better but I have to develop more study habits than I have. I really want to bring those grades up but as of now, it's satisfactory, but I could do a lot better.

Q: What factors do you identify as contributing to your success?

A: Well, I contribute my success to mainly my grandmother and my mother because they kept me, I could have been doing a lot of other things, bad things, but they kept me in the church and kept me busy with Optimist football and basketball, things of that nature, so by them keeping me on the right track, and by me being involved with other people who I looked up to and who expected good things from me, I didn't want to let them down, I didn't want to let my mother down, and I didn't want to let my grandmother down, so those are the things that kept me on the right track.

Q: What did you see in the neighborhood that could have prevented you from getting to college at this point in your life?

A: Well, the things that I have been exposed to were, at the time I was in school, I had a little, decent job but I was exposed to seeing things some of my friends who did some negative things that they accumulated a lot of money fast and I could have went that route but those are some of the things that I really saw a lot of, and it's kinda hard when you are young—you want those kinda things in life but, you know, by me being in the church and listening to my grandmother, you know, patience, believe in God, and be patient and things will work out, don't go for the fast money and all that kinda of stuff 'cause it's not gonna last forever, so those were the things I was exposed to.

Q: And you listened to your grandmother?

A: Definitely, definitely, I listened to my grandmother 'cause I didn't want to let her down and I felt that I just had to be on my P's and Q's because I felt that at a young age, she had me kinda brainwashed thinking that she could see everything that I did, so that kinda kept me on the right track also.

Q: What factors do you identify that could have been obstacles to your success?

A: Like I said earlier, the negative things that went on in my neighborhood. There were a lot of drug dealings going on. Some of my friends did drugs. I remember when I was in high school, we had some guys in class doing drugs right in the classroom, so those things could have easily got me on the wrong track 'cause those were my friends, but I knew right from wrong at that time, so I stayed on my track and they stayed on their track, but, you know, I never did forget them as friend—they were still my friends but they decided to do that and I decided to do my thing, so it worked out for the best. I'm glad I chose the route that I chose.

Q: What courses of action did you take to overcome the obstacles that you encountered?

A: Well, by me having a love for sports, most of the time when my friends were doing these negative things, I would take it upon myself to go to the court and play some games of basketball, go to the park and play some football, things of that nature, and if I wasn't interested in sports, then that could have easily been my hobby so to speak—those negatives things, but my hobby was sports. I was very sports oriented, so that kinda kept me on the right track as far as staying out of trouble.

Q: What were the major influences in your life?

A: First of all, like I said, my grandmother and my mother had a major influence in my life. But then my mom got me into this Big Brother/Big Sister program and I had a big brother. Even though I'm black, he was a Jewish, white male. I thought that was a real turning thing 'cause I learned a little bit about his culture and he learned a little bit about mine. I was glad that he took it upon himself to have a black kid as a Little Brother. He could have had a Little Brother who was white, but he chose to have one that was black, and I learned a lot of things from him, as far as just everyday manners, you know, not to litter, and, you know, treat people as you would like them to treat you, and just little things that he instilled in me to make me a better person, and to this day I still think about those things that he taught me.

Q: Do you in return have a Little Brother?

A: Well, I have biological brothers but by me playing all these, I'm playing sports and I'm a senior now, it's hard to really reach down and spend a lot of time with a smaller, younger person even though I would like to and eventually I will, but right now I'm trying to get myself together and I do sometimes spend time with a few guys in my family who are kind of on the verge of doing bad things, but I can't spend as much time as I would like to by the things that I'm involved in right now.

Q: Were your teachers major influences?

A: Yeah, my teachers were a good influence. Like I said, they taught me the book knowledge and also they taught me how to cope once I got out of high school, and they are teaching me now how to cope once I get out of college, so they are very influential in helping me become a whole person, not just book knowledge but street knowledge and things about life in general—business and things of that nature.

Q: Were your peers a major influence?

A: Well, pretty much. Most of my peers, I guess you can say that some of them were and some of them weren't. Most of the time I was really kept to myself. I had a few friends who I call good friends, but I was really my own person. No one could really influence me to do something that I didn't want to do, but I kinda kept company with those persons who had the same interests that I had, so it was really easy for us to get along because we had pretty much the same interest.

Q: And was the church a major influence in your life?

A: Very much so because once I'm in the church a lot, you know, people in the church seem to get caught up in what you're doing and how you're doing, and what are you're doing with yourself because when they see a young person, a young adult going to church on a regular basis, they kinda get interested in what's going on in your life, so after a lot of people got interested in me, to myself I said, well, I can't do anything bad to let them down, I can't do anything bad to let my grandmother down, so that kinda kept me going. When things got a little rough, that kept me going, knowing that I wouldn't want to see their faces if I was to get in trouble, go to jail or something like that.

Q: And who were your role models?

A: I would say my Big Brother, Bob, and my mother and my grandmother, and some of the coaches that I've had when I was playing Optimist sports. They really taught me things that still stay with me today.

Q: Did you have any relationship with your father?

A: Well, no. I grew up in a single-family home; it was me, my mother and my grandmother, and I guess you can say my grandmother served as the father role but my father was really absent in my life when I needed him, you know, when I was young, I needed a father role but he was absent. Even though he wasn't there, I don't have anything against him, you know, I really don't see him that much today but right now, at this point in my life, I don't really need a father now, but he wasn't there for me when I was young, but my mother and my grandmother made accommodations for me to get those male role models that I needed when my father wasn't there.

Q: And who served as the role models then?

A: Some of the coaches that I've had when I was playing Optimist football, my mom, my grandmother, my Big Brother from the Big Brother/Big Sisters program, and a few of my teachers that I've had, and some of the friends of the family.

Q: How did you get into the Big Brothers/Little Brothers program?

A: Big Brother/Little Sisters, something like that, program, and what it was, my mom, I don't know, she just got me signed up with it and then they matched, they put your name on some kind of sheet and then whoever is interested in being your Big Brother, they respond to the ad, and I guess my mom put the ad out and then the guy, Bob, responded and then we just started. It's like a weekly thing—you go out at least once a week and you keep contact with your Little Brother by either a telephone call or you go out and do things and it went real well. We did things—we did a lot of things together. I spent the night over to his house, I met his mom, I saw how the Jewish faith does things, you know, it was a real good experience, and I would recommend it to anybody, any young kid who needs a male model in their life.

Q: How long did it last?

A: It lasted approximately two, maybe a year, and then he was in the stage where I'm at now where he wanted to enhance himself and go to college, so then he, I think at the time he was going to college then he got a lucrative job offer in New York, so he had to go ahead and move on and enhance his life, so I think it lasted approximately one year.

Q: And how old were you at the time?

A: I think I was around nine, ten, or eleven years old at the time, around that age.

Q: And it was impressionable for you?

A: Very much so, very much so. He instilled in me a lot of things that I had that I wasn't even aware of, and the things I remember the most, you know, when we went to eat somewhere, then after I finished I just threw the paper out the car and he said, "Don't do that," because the only things you throw out the window are things that nature will—anything that is biodegradable, such as fruits, things that is not paper or stuff would not degrade, so that would be detrimental to the environment, so he made me very aware of how the environment is and things that would hurt the environment and things that would help the environment.

Q: You spoke about athletics. How did they influence your life?

A: Athletics had a major influence in my life. One of the major good things about it was it did keep me out of trouble and kept me busy, and I learned a lot of things about discipline and teamwork and how to work well with others, and things of that nature. If it wasn't for athletics, I probably wouldn't be in college today.

Q: How did athletics get you into school?

A: Me and a friend of mine would always go down and play at this local gym in the neighborhood and there was a guy there who was a former graduate of FM College. He played basketball here and he saw that me and this guy was young, we played ball, and we had talent, so he asked me, "What are you guys doing with yourself?" well, you know, we're just working, come and play ball once in a while. He said, "Well, I can get you in college if you're really interested in going." So we really didn't take him seriously, but, you know, we said okay, whatever, so eventually, we talked and he kept pursuing us, so we said this guy must be serious, so eventually he brought us to the college, FM, and he introduced us to the coach and showed us around and told us that if we were really interested in coming, we can go ahead and sign up, pick our classes and we can start the following semester. So before I knew it, I was in college. I won a basketball scholarship because of this guy noticing me and because of sports, I'm playing sports, and being at the right place and the right time, good things happen.

Q: And how do you see that as being important to your continuing development?

A: Well, that was a start and I know that good things are bound to happen, are bound to appear again, because I involve myself with positive people and only good things can come out of that, because I really try not to hang with people who are negative, because only negative things can come from that, so I involve myself with positive people and goods things happen. Of course, with belief in God and trust in God, good things happen.

Q: What organizations can you identify as being important to your development?

A: Well, first of all, the Big Brother/Big Sister organization—that was real influential, the Optimist Clubs in the local area in the neighborhood—that really helped me out a great deal and being in the church—that really helped me out. I was in the "Youth Expressing Christ." That was a church group for teenagers at my church. And those were basically the influential groups that I had myself in to help enhance me and make me a better person.

Q: You belong to a fraternity?

A: Yes.

Q: Kappa Alpha?

A: Yes, Kappa Alpha Psi Fraternity, Inc.

Q: Does that contribute to your success, or how was it important to you?

A: What that is, I became interested in the fraternities when I came out to the college. I noticed how they come together and do certain things, and the colors and the step shows and everything like that, but it's not all about the step shows, it's about helping people in the community, and the reason that I joined Kappa Alpha Psi is because I observed all the fraternities on campus and they were the ones who seemed to be more influential and helped the community, and because of that, that's why I made a choice of Kappa Alpha Psi, and by me being in that fraternity, it teaches me how to conduct myself as a gentleman, how to handle business, how to take care of, just to be a man, and overall taking care of business, reaching back and helping young kids, and just doing things that need to be done in the community.

Q: How long have you been a member of The President's Men's program?

A: It has been two years since I've been a member.

Q: How have you participated?

A: Well, as of now, my participation has been little, not as much as it should be because I'm busy with basketball all the time and when they do have meetings I'm involved in my classes but when I have time I do stop by and give my input on some of the situations that have arose and The President's Men and Kappa Alpha Psi is kinda along the same accordance because they are both organizations that enhance young men and help them be better role models and persons as a whole.

Q: Do you feel these kinds of organizations are important because of role models and mentorships?

A: Yes. First of all, I feel that they are very important because it brings men together for a common goal, and that's to help the community, to uplift yourself as a person, and to teach you how to work well with others, so it's very influential in helping the development of a young black man.

Q: What can you as a successful student at a historically black college recommend or advise young black males?

A: There's a lot of things I can advise or tell black males because there are so many things out there now that can detour their attention from education. There's lots of ways to get quick money, lots of ways to do this and do that, but you have to be patient and realize that education is the best way to get the better things out of life instead of some of these other things that are going on today, and being at a black college, a historically black college, and by it being a small college, the classrooms are very small and you get one-on-one attention from your instructors and its like a close-knit environment. It's very enjoyable, very helpful too, I feel.

Q: How do you advise them to take the first step toward going to college?

A: Well, first you have to have a interest in wanting to educate yourself and then you have to take it upon yourself to write certain schools or visit the schools in your area and see what kind of requirements that you need to have met from high school to enable you to be available to go to college, so it takes a little self-work to get started, but once you get started, you know, you have to be persistent and keep trying, and then good things will happen.

Q: What is inside you that motivates you to succeed?

A: Well, when I see my mother and my grandmother, how they—they didn't really struggle but they really worked hard to get me the things that I needed out of life and when I see that I feel I want to make life for them better. They took chances and helped bring me up right, so I want to reward them for bringing me up right, and I have a little sister now [mother's child] and I look at her and her father is not in the picture like my father was, so I play the role of my mother, and my grandmother's grandson, son, grandfather, little brother, big brother, so I play all those roles and I can't let them down. I have to keep on going and sometimes when I get tired, I think of them, I have to keep going and push myself so I can be a person to them so I can take care of them sometimes, so they can relax for all the good work they've done in bringing me up.

Q: What passes through your thoughts when you have to make a decision?

A: Lots of things goes through my mind. I often think, when I make decisions, I often think how the other person would feel in the decision I make because I really can't go out and just hurt another person for no apparent reason, so when I make decisions I think I look at the whole picture, how would this decision affect this person, how is this going to affect me, is this the best decision for me, is this the best decision to not affect this other person, so I look at the whole picture before I make any decision.

Q: Would you like to share any other thoughts before we close the interview?

A: Well, I would like to say that being in college, I felt if I have enough faith in God, good things happen to you, you be at the right place and the right time, and good things happen to you. I was on the verge of being a bad seed so to speak but by my grandmother and my mother keeping me in those positive things, that really kept me out of trouble, and when you think positive, positive things can happen, so I recommend that any young person go to church—hear the Word. Even though I'm a religious person, I don't run around with a Bible in my hand all the time trying to convert people, you know, I have my own faith, I have it inside me and I pray at night, but I don't really run around flaunting it like some people do, but I am a religious person and I just say think positive thoughts and positive things will happen.

OBSERVER'S COMMENTS

Respondent:

- is 6 feet 3 inches, 160 pounds;
- most people "think of him as quiet, shy," not outgoing, but personable when introduced to people;
- didn't feel a sense of loss because father was not at home;
- had strong guidance from grandmother; she worked with special needs people and respondent had experience with these people, as grandmother brought him to the center, where grandmother was a teacher (graduated from high school);
- mother's college degree from Florida International University; works at Florida Power Light.

INTERVIEW 34

Q: Who lived in your home with you as you were growing up?

A: My mother and my grandmother were the only two that lived at home with me.

Q: Can you describe the house that you grew up in?

A: The house that I grew up in had a lot of love. There were only two women in the house, and I was the only young man in the house, and sometimes it would be a little rough not having a father image in the household, but in that house, those two women reared a young man that has a lot of love on the inside of him.

Q: How many bedrooms did you have in your home?

A: We lived in an apartment, and it was an apartment that had one bedroom, and then we moved from that apartment, living in the same complex, to another one that had three bedrooms and two bathrooms.

Q: Did you grow up in Miami?

A: I lived in Miami all of my life. I'm twenty years old now, and I lived part of that twenty years here, being reared in Miami.

Q: What section of Miami did you grow up in?

A: I grew up in Liberty City, which is probably well known by a lot of people—professional people, people of all races and colors—all know about Liberty City.

Q: Could you describe your neighborhood?

A: My neighborhood was drug infested, welfare parents, a lot of older people, and it was one of really not much joy, but it was a neighborhood.

Q: Did you have many friends in that neighborhood?

A: In that neighborhood, I had a lot of friends. I had a lot of young male friends, most of them who were not much of a good influence, but, because of having common sense, I survived.

Q: Was your family on welfare?

A: No, my family was not on welfare. My grandmother worked, and she worked doing days work [housework], and other things, and my mother worked for Pan Am—the airport, and then it closed, and she became employed with the Dade County Public School Board, working in the cafeteria.

Q: In the previous answer, you mentioned "drug infested." How did you keep safe in an environment like that?

A: I kept safe from that mainly through common sense, as I said, because most kids have common sense, but they don't use it. I was able to look, at a very young age, and see that if I took drugs or something, I saw what it did to "John," then I knew what could happen to me, and, basically, through common sense, and through my family constantly talking to me, constantly being with me, I survived, I really did. It's amazing, but I really did—I survived it through common sense and through the communication with my family. We had open communication. We were able to talk, and, basically, being able to see everyone fall around you, and you're the only one standing, it's a blessing.

Q: When you came home from school were you allowed to go outside to play?

A: When I came home from school, I was free to do basically whatever it is that I wanted to do. I was able to go see the neighbors. I was free to go see my friends, and we had a pretty liberated home. Basically, during most of my childhood, my mother, worked at the airport, so I would have to go stay with my grandfather at my father's home, and over there, I would stay most of the evening, and play with the kids in that neighborhood, and then my grandmother would come from work, and pick me up, and I would stay over, until my mom got home from work. So, basically, I walked from school every day, to my grandmom's house, and I stayed there, and from there, I would go home, so I had a lot of freedom to do my homework, and then, after my homework was complete, to go out and play with other kids.

Q: What neighborhood did your grandmother and grandfather live in?

A: My grandmother and my grandfather lived also in Liberty City. They just lived in another vicinity—another area, but it was the same community, and the community that they pretty much lived in was the same; it was infested, too, with drugs, not as bad as where I lived. It wasn't as known, but my grandmother, they lived in a house, and it was across the street from a complex—governmental complex, so, basically, I would have my cousins to play with, and then the kids over in the complex to play with, whom I went to school with, by the way.

Q: Was your grandfather a role model?

A: Oh, my grandfather was a beautiful role model—a beautiful man. He took me fishing, and he took me to do things that I didn't get to do—living with two women in the household, in my household. My grandfather, he worked for the city, cutting trees for Metro-Dade for a long time. He's retired now. He was a beautiful role model even up until now, he still is.

Q: Are you speaking about two grandmothers, one grandmother that lived with you, and one grandmother that lived in another apartment or home?

A: Yes. One, my mother's mother, she's divorced—she's divorced from my mother's father, and my father's mother and father were married, and they have been married now for about fifty years—fifty-seven, fifty-something-odd years, and, basically, it's like it was two different environments: one was a family environment and the other one was—it was both really family environments—but the other one was kind of different, you know, you felt the difference in the home environment.

Q: What would that difference be?

A: The difference in the other environment would be seeing my grandmother prepare meals and take care of the kids that were living in her house, sit down and talk to her husband when he comes from work, and see them talk about family issues, family things that would generate, or that would come across the table, basically, things that married couples talk about and families go through in a married couple's home, than in a single-parent's home.

Q: What kind of interactions transpired at your home, your mother's home?

A: In my mother's home, my grandmother is a very dear woman. My mother had me at a very young age, and my grandmother was the type in our home, and even now, she handles everything. She has the business smarts. She has the sense of how to take care of things and do everything; whereas my mother, she was like a young girl who, at the time, made a lot of mistakes and now, you know, she looks back and says, "Oh, I wish I had done this and done that," but my grandmother, on the other hand, was the type that if she had a chance, she went to school, she did whatever she could do, so basically, in my household what transpired was more of like learning, being taught, me and my mother both being taught by my grandmother, how to live in this life, and how to survive and how to make it.

Q: How old was your mother when she gave birth to you?

A: When my mother had me, my mother was sixteen years old, and she was in the ninth grade, my father was a senior getting ready to graduate, and my mother was a freshman, and she used to tell me how she used to get up and get ready for school, get me ready and then drop me off to the babysitter, and then go to school, and she successfully completed high school, and with many more opportunities to go on to school, she didn't go because she was the type, my mother was the type, she needs to be encouraged, also, so it's kind of different when you're used to someone encouraging you, but then, in turn, you have to turn around and say, "Mom, this is how you do this, and this is the way it's supposed to go, and this is what you should do," so it's kind of different. It feels funny—it's different.

Q: Were you and your mother almost like sister and brother?

A: Very much, very much. We were like sister and brother, and I didn't begin calling my mother "mom" until about, gosh, maybe, oh gosh, maybe later on in elementary. I would always call her by her first name, Vivian, you know, and then it kind of grew on me. I would say, "Hey, mom," you know, "mom, mom," and I call her mom now, so. . . .

Q: What did you call your grandmother when you were growing up?

A: Ever since birth, "Grandmother." She's always been Grandma—Grandma, you know, I call her grandma, never called her by her first name ever, and even now, today, it's Grandma. Every time, I call her Grandma.

Q: Did you have any kind of relationship with your father?

A: I did. My father is incarcerated, and he's in prison now, and before my father went off to prison, he came over, and he was telling me that he loved me, and he loved me, and I didn't know what was going on. And before, we had a relationship but it got cut off. When we began to really see each other and began to understand each other, this is when the incident happened in his life and it kind of—it was like a big chain, a bit split, and my father, his birthday, I think it will be Wednesday, he'll be forty years old. I'm twenty, he's forty—we're about twenty years, I guess twenty years apart from each other, and I don't know, we had a good relationship. He wanted to do things for me, and just when he began to do things for me, things went—just erupted, and he was sent to some part of Florida, so we keep in contact, not as much, I've seen him about three times. He sees me. He sees the accomplishments that I have made in my life, and it's amazing to know that you can grow up without a father, but there are some consequences that happened later on in life that you really regret, and you wish that you did have a father in the household.

Q: What do you feel that you have missed in not having a father in the household?

A: Oh, my gosh, I missed that love from a man's point of view, having the male figure in the household just to say, "Hey, Dad," or someone to hug you, or to be there with you in those times when you really need him. Most young men are taught—some fathers that live at home with their sons, maybe they'll tuggle with them, or play with them, or something, and those are the things that a young male needs, because what happens is he doesn't have that love at a young age, and what happens is it comes back—I think it comes back as a distorted love, which turns into the love—where it's turned into something perverse, and, I think, that is what's happening to a lot of black men, too, and males period, in this country. It comes back as a form of homosexuality, because they didn't get the love at home, or what they would get from their father, so it comes back years later, but it comes back distorted, and I think that that's the part that's real sad, but if you could escape all of that, to me, you're blessed, you know, but a father's love is so important, because when you talk to many young men, and you try to tell them, because I'm involved in the church, and you try to tell them about their father, you say, the father as in Christ, and it's hard to tell them something about a father, because they can't identify when you haven't had a father to support you, you haven't had a father to be there for you, you haven't had a father to love you, but then you try to tell them that Christ loves you, you know, he loves you, he's there, but then the male figure is missing in the home, so they can't identify with that concept. They don't understand.

Q: How would you define success?

A: Success. My goodness. My true definition of success—the world gives you a definition as being the American Dream, a car—a nice car, a nice house, an education, you name it, I guess eating at the best restaurants, wearing the best clothing and doing those types of things, but my definition of good success is when you have the Lord, Jesus, in your life, and when you just have the Word, the wisdom of God, because to me, I don't care how intelligent you are—someone that does not have a mind of God, sometimes it's a lot of distractions and distortions coming in—but to me, good success is knowing Christ.

Q: How old were you when you came to that definition of success?

A: That definition didn't come along until—it was always there when I was young—and having a very painful child-life a little bit—and to know that I survived, Oh, my gosh, it didn't become real prominent until I came to college, and I met some young people that God had truly blessed me to be with, and I began to find out what having good success is, and having and knowing that terminology—the definition I just gave you—that truly is success, because what happens is, the world—what they do is they offer you, you know, you can go to a masseuse and you can get a massage, and they'll offer you every other thing, and say, I have a bad day, I'll lay on the table, I'll get a massage, but when I get up from that table, I'll be the same me that laid down there to get that massage, and nothing would have changed, nothing would have sparked me, because, to me, you just stay the same, you know, with that American Dream—the car, the house, and all those things—and some people have all those things, and they're still not happy, and they're still not—they feel like they haven't accomplished whatever it is they're looking for, but I have a concept that says never be satisfied, which is—never be comfortable or satisfied, never settle for less, but always reach toward those things, those high goals—those high promises.

Q: Based on your grade-point average, would you say that you are a successful student?

A: Based on my GPA, would I say that I am a successful student? Oh, yuck. In a way, looking from my perspective, I would say that I am a successful student still reaching to go on higher heights, to go deeper in my education and my thrust for education. Sometimes, I look at the philosophies of a lot of philosophers who left their definition of what they felt about education, and one was a lady by the name of Mary McCloud Bethune. She was saying how she leaves her peace; she leaves her racial dignities; and she leaves her thrust for education; she leaves her hunger for knowledge to the young people, and when I look at that philosophy of education, that's kind of what I base my success on at this college, trying to hold on to that will and testament that she left, that I may have a hunger for education and a desire to do the right thing, and, basically, that's my documentary for that question.

Q: What factors do you identify as contributing to your success?

A: The factors that I identify with contributing to my success—a true factor is running into a dynamic group of men, dynamic group of people that have sat me down and talked to me and said, "Hey, look." I had a counselor that sat me down and talked to me and told me, "You know, don't feel bad, because you're different or because you're looked upon as different, because later on, many of those people will come back and want to know what it is that you did, because I was always a quiet person. I was always a humble person—very humble, very lowly, very meek, never had much to say, and I think the skills that attributed to my success has been the humbleness, the lowliness, and the meekness, and those characteristics, that's what I would say has contributed to my success, and hard work, and dedication, and commitment. No one wants to make a commitment, and I've met a lot of short-term people. They come in, and after that, it's like if things don't go their way, then they leave, or if they can't change something that comes their way, then they leave, but I think commitment, making a commitment to stay no matter what it is, no matter what happens and no matter what anyone says, but it's a commitment to this institution, to my life, and, basically, I think those are the factors that I can identify toward contributing to my success.

Q: What did the counselor mean when he said "different"? In what way did he see you as being different?

A: When I was in high school, we termed different as being called a "nerd," never being with the "in crowd"; never being able to fit in, never being the one where young ladies would come to your house and say, "Let's go out for a burger or something." A good example—Mr. S— when he was in college, it was the same way. When he was in high school, it was the same way, and when he got to college, it was even more like that. He was never in with the "in crowd." And, finally, when college was over, he became a very successful man, and most of those people that didn't want to be with him, and did not want to have anything to do with him—finally, it's paid off—my gosh, he can go on a lot and just pay for a Mercedes Benz in cash, if he wanted to, but that's not the type of person he is. He's been a real father figure—beautiful, he and his wife, beautiful people. So when he said "different," that's what he meant—never fit in with the "in crowd," never have any of those characteristics to be with the "in crowd people," and I've never had them—never, never had them.

Q: Do you see yourself as a "nerd"?

A: More so now, more than I would want to be; I don't know what you call it now, but I would like to be called an intelligent nerd, or whatever, or I would love to be that term now. I think that's the best thing to be called in this hour, in this day, in this age that we live in, but I would say, I would kinda say, Yeah, they would probably say I'm the nerd type, because I don't go out to parties, and I'm not the partying type, but I do know some nerds that do party, but that word, "nerd," has a wide definition today—very wide. There are some nerds that are jocks. You can't tell. You just don't know. Today, you don't know.

Q: What factors do you identify that could have been obstacles to your success?

A: Factors that could have been obstacles to my success could have been laziness, could have been probably the drug-infested environment—it probably could have been a factor, the largest factor that I determine that could have been an obstacle could have been laziness. I wouldn't say, one factor I would surely not say that could have stopped me is the talk of people and what people had to say about me, or whatnot, having the support of people, because I don't care. People don't make you, I mean, sometimes it hurts what people say, yes, it does sometimes, but we always used to have a saying, "The pen is mightier than the sword," but I would even say the pen is mightier than someone's mouth, but I would think that if I had been lazy and received all those things that people had to say, then that would have been one main obstacle that could have stopped, but other than that, there's nothing impossible and nothing that can stop you.

I believe that my motto is, "Only you can stop yourself—no one else can stop you—only you can."

Q: If you came across an obstacle, how would you overcome it?

A: If I came across an obstacle . . . ?

Q: What course of action would you take?

A: The course of action that I would take, and that I'm taking now, is I'm kind of speaking to a lot of the obstacles that I'm in, meeting them head on, because sometimes I go find, and I'll run smack into a wall, and sometimes it seems like these walls are hard to get over or to come by, but, eventually, I think that facing up to a lot of these walls, sometimes the walls can be yourself, and a lot of these things are hard to face up, but I'm learning to face straight ahead of, into these walls and confront them straight on, and speak to some of these obstacles that are in our way, and confront them head on. Some of them are nasty, some of them are ugly, but I think that if you face them head on, identify the problem and after you identify the obstacle, maybe do a little research, and when you find out about your enemy, whatever it is that's stopping you, when you do a little research on it and find out what it is, and you can use some knowledge to kinda counterattack it, you know, hit it in its weak point.

Q: Were there major influences in your life—you mentioned your family, and you mentioned counselors—were there teachers?

A: I had this one teacher who graduated from Fisk University with a degree in mathematics, and I was poor in math. I really had a tough time in math, and this teacher, he helped me out a lot. He was patient, he was loving, he was kind, and all the things that a teacher should possess, and because of him, I've grasped a lot of my math skills now, and I've learned a lot of things in math. There's so many role models—so many people. If I had to pull them out of my bag, I mean, it's hard to find a role model now, even though there are so many, and we kind of use the television. I hate using television for role models. I don't like it. I think it's demoralizing now to look at television. It kinda breaks your character down to sit there and look at that stuff and pick a role model off of that television, but my highest role model, I would personally kind of say is—my family's been good. I won't forget the little people that pitched in, the teachers and family, of course, the church has been a role model, but within myself deeply, I try to look for that potential within myself that's lying dormant, kinda chose that to be the role model, and I must say there are some things that are inside of me that I really didn't know, that I still don't know, but that I'm tapping into, to find out that a lot of those things are becoming my role model.

Q: What is it inside you that motivates you to succeed? Can you explain it?

A: Potential, you know, everyone says oh, I have potential—potential, and I look at potential, I look at the word "potential," as being that which is hidden, that is lying dormant, that that you haven't tapped into, and I would say that some of the dormant potential that I know, I can't wake up, but I won't use the word "can't" but that it "could" be wakened up, but it's gonna take everything within me—it's gonna take everything on the inside of me to wake up that potential—sometimes in order to wake up that potential that's dormant, you have to drop a lot of things, take off a lot of things, maybe refrain from certain people, stay from around certain people.

Q: Were you at all involved in athletics as an influence in your life?

A: Oh, my gosh, I was never athletic, but I always did intramural sports, playing with kids.

Q: Are activities and organizations that you can identify as being important to your continuing development?

A: The activities and organizations that I feel that helps me continue in my development has been President's Men, of course, has been one of those things that were beautiful when our first president had gotten here, and it still is beautiful, because he really wanted us to continue out his dream, and his dream of The President's Men was to get black young men to participate in networking in communication skills because a lot of our communication skills were poor and networking with other companies and other people like Kelloggs and AT&T, and his dream was setting up an alliance where we could get together with these companies and develop a friendship, sort of like a bond with each other and to keep a dream within the inside of us alive to go out into these companies, and to kind of set up a network with these guys and kind of learn the networking process, to learn skills from each other, not sort so much of money, but to just learn skills, what it's like to work in a company, what it's like to be an executive or CEO, you know—what did they do, what are the skills—are you the one that hires the guys that work for you and determine a lot of things, or what is it that it's like, and the Pre-Alumni Association here has been beautiful—that organization has been beautiful. It's a money-marketing organization for the college, getting the alumni to pay the bills and donate back to the college, that has been a beautiful continuing development of helping me. I go over there and talk to the chairperson over there and she's beautiful; she's young, she graduated from Howard University, and she did it in four years—four years flat, with a degree in communications, and I was learning how did that tie in with the Pre-Alumni, and that helped me out a lot, also. So those are continuing things that helped me also.

Q: What reasons are these activities and organizations important to you?

A: They're important because, what happens is I enjoy being where I am now because I get to see other leaders, because one day I may be in their shoes and I may be a leader, and I get to see what it is that they do, how do they work under pressure not having help, not having any help come in and seeing how they think, "How am I going to raise all of this money? I have to have so much allocated for the college and I have to do it under all this amount of pressure—alone," and it's like seeing people kind of work under pressure, seeing other people's dream and not being the dream killer, but seeing them dream the impossible and using myself to help it come true, and knowing that I'm a part of it, to know that you're a part of someone else's dream is beautiful, because it lets you know that they're thinking about you, and that really is important to me and it helps me to know that someone cares and knowing that someone else wants to help and if I could be of help to someone else, it's beautiful, and that's important to me. These activities and organizations show that type of criteria. They have that ability and it's beautiful to me.

Q: What can you, as a successful student at a historically black college, recommend or advise young black males?

A: I would advise young black males when they come to this, when they go to a historically black college, whether it be here, or in Atlanta, or wherever it is, or wherever state they go to, I would advise them to go with their own dream, not Dr. King's dream, but go with your own dream. We don't have any dreamers anymore that dream the impossible, you know—dream of having your own school, have these dreams, and I guarantee you they'll come true, maybe if you have a dream of having children being healed when they come to your school by the love that you possess—dream that, and know that you can, you could bring that to pass, and know that it could happen just by your belief and by your contributions and the things that you would do to make that dream come alive.

It's time to have a fresh dream on the inside of us, individually. That's what I recommend to a black male—have your own dream—one that you could reach.

Q: Could you add anything to that if you were speaking to young black males in the community?

A: I would tell black young males not only to dream the impossible, but I would also tell them to have work. Work so that if you were cooking french fries, you know, be the best french-fry cooker, have a plan, have a plan A and a plan B, and if plan A and plan B doesn't work, don't stop there—continue to work, desire to have an education, desire to want to be different, and work towards it like never before, and don't stop, don't give up, because I've run into some obstacles, and I've run into some things that seemed unbearable, and some things that usually come back to say, "Hey, I'm here, you thought I was gone," but you can do it, they can do it. We've had so many clouds of witnesses that have done it, and I know that it can be done. It truly can be done. The little that I've done has been a blessing to me. It's been great to me. And I would tell black males that it's amazing what you can do when you elevate your mind, when you elevate yourself above that what you're in. Elevation is beautiful because it's progressive, you keep going a ladder higher and higher—people don't understand that but I would tell them to go for the gusto.

Q: What is inside you that motivates you to succeed?

A: My endurance and my strength. People normally tell me that "Oh, K, you're so slow, you're like an old man," and I really think it's beautiful to have an old man's wisdom in a young man's body. You don't run into a lot of that today. Not only do I feel good sometimes, but I also think—it's good to think good. It's good to think above those things, you know, I don't look at how long I've been without, or what I don't have, but I really look at where I'm going to, not what I'm going through. I look at where I'm going to, because I know that it's gonna pay off after awhile. Waiting is a problem for a lot of young people—male or female—it's waiting, it's like I have to have it now, you know, can I have the Jaguar now, can I get it now, but if you wait, you know, it will come to pass. Come high or low, it will come to pass; I'm a witness, it will come to pass.

Q: When you have to make a decision, what thoughts pass through your mind?

A: Being a decision maker is not hard, but I learned that if you're gonna do something you have to have a made-up mind and you have to have a determination. Many people don't care about your determination in this day and hour but you, yourself, have to be determined and know I made this decision and I'm gonna stick to it, and so many things run through my mind, because you the decision that you make could either destroy you or it can make you, it can uplift you or it can deter you. There's so many things that run through my mind, but if I make the wrong decision, because I know that I'm redeemed, when I say "redeemed," I mean that I can—I'm redeemed from poverty, you know; it's like how do you tell somebody that you're redeemed from poverty, and it's like "Look, K, I'm in poverty"—to me, being a decision maker is a part of being a leader, and we don't have a lot of people that want to be leaders because of the decisions that we have to make on a day-to-day basis, but I would just say when I make my decision, I'll just say I take the consequences that comes along with it. It's like jumping out on thin air, and to me, that's sometimes what you have to do—you have to make a decision. Who was it, Robert Townsend made a decision. He charged up a credit card of $1 million, made movies on credits cards, and did not know what was going to be the decision of that movie—what was going to happen, but so happened that movie paid back and now

Robert Townsend is a star and he paid off those million-dollar credit cards, but if I had to talk to him and say what prompted you to make that decision, I don't know what he'd tell me.

Q: Would you like to share any other thoughts before we close the interview on the subject matter of success factors?

A: I'm just glad to be of help to this. I think it's beautiful. I've learned a lot from it. Success is wide-range and I would just say that success lies within the person, what you think about it. I don't look at success the way the world looks at it, or the way the president would come up with a plan of being successful because we do know that having your own home, having your own car is not good—we've seen these people commit suicide and we've seen them kill others, but it goes much deeper. It goes very, very, very much deeper than what "the way the world pictures it to be." It's deep. It's very deep.

OBSERVER'S COMMENTS

Respondent:

- is a gentle person, religious orientation;
- had a sense of wisdom for a twenty-year-old that amazed me;
- is a good listener, articulate and believable;
- remarked, "I'm a thoroughbred man";
- said that he resembled his father, and when he saw the resemblance, it upset him.

References

Allen, W. R. (1992). "African-American College Student Outcomes at Predominantly White and Historically Black Public Colleges and Universities." *Harvard Educational Review*, 62 (1), 26–44.

Ascher, C. (1991). *School Programs for African-American Male Students: Trends and Issues*. Washington, DC: Office of Educational Research and Improvement. (ERIC Document Reproduction Service No. ED 334938).

Billingsley, A. (1992). *Climbing Jacob's Ladder: The Enduring Legacy of African-American Families*. New York: Simon & Schuster.

"Black-White Higher Education Equality Index." (1993). *The Journal of Blacks in Higher Education* (1), 16–24.

"Black-White Higher Education Equality Index." (1996, Autumn). *The Journal of Blacks in Higher Education*, 66–69.

Booker, S. (1988, July). "Black General at the Summit of U.S. Power." *Ebony*, 136–137, 144, 146.

Bowser, B. P. (ed.). (1991). *Black Male Adolescents: Parenting and Education in Community Context*. Lanham, MD: University Press of America.

Bowser, B. P., and Perkins, H. (1991). "Success Against the Odds: Young Black Men Tell What It Takes." In B. P. Bowser (Ed.), *Black Male Adolescents: Parenting and Education in Community Context*. Lanham, MD: University Press of America.

Carnoy, M. (1994/1995, Winter). "Aren't More African Americans Going to College?" *The Journal of Blacks in Higher Education*, 66–69.

Castenell, L. (1984). "A Cross-Cultural Look at Achievement Motivation Research." *Journal of Negro Education*, 53 (4), 435–443.

Cheatham, H. E., and Stewart, J. B. (1993). *Black Families*. New Brunswick, NJ: Transaction.

Clark, R. (1983). *Family Life and School Achievement: Why Poor Black Children Succeed or Fail*. Chicago: University of Chicago Press.

Collins, P. H. (1991). "The Meaning of Motherhood in Black Culture." In R. Staples (Ed.), *The Black Family. Essays and Studies*. Belmont, CA: Wadsworth.

Crabtree, B., and Miller, W. L. (eds.). (1992). *Doing Qualitative Research*. Newbury Park, CA: Sage.

DuBois, W.E.B. (1961). *The Souls of Black Folk*. Greenwich, CT: Fawcett. (Original work published 1903.)

Edwards, A., and Polite, C. K. (1992). *Children of the Dream: The Psychology of Black Success*. New York: Doubleday.

Elam, J. C. (ed.). (1989). *Blacks in Higher Education: Overcoming the Odds*. A NAFEO Research Institute Publications. Lanham, MD: University Press of America.

Elam, J. D., Ugbah, S. D., and Williams, S. A. (eds.). (1989). "The Mentor-Protégé Relationship: Its Impact on the Academic and Career Development of Blacks in Predominantly White Institutions." NAFEO Research Institute, University Press of America.

Ellison, R. (1952). *The Invisible Man*. New York: Random House.

Embler, W. (1966). *Metaphor and Meaning*. De Land, FL: Everett/Edwards.

Feagin, J., Vera, H., and Imani, N. (1996). *The Agony of Education, Black Students at White Colleges and Universities*. New York: Routledge.

Fleming, J. (1991). *Blacks in College*. San Francisco: Jossey-Bass.

Forcey, L. R. (1987). *Mothers of Sons: Toward an Understanding of Responsibility*. New York: Praeger.

Garibaldi, A. M. (1992). "Educating and Motivating African American Males to Succeed." *Journal of Negro Education*, 61 (1), 4–11.

Glaser, B. G., and Strauss, A. L. (1965). "The Purpose and Credibility of Qualitative Research." *Nursing Research*, 15 (1), 56–61.

Glaser, B. G., and Strauss, A. L. (1967). *The Discovery of Grounded Theory*. Chicago: Aldine.

Gosman, E. J., Dandridge, B. A., Nettles, M. T., and Thoeny, A. R. (1982). *Predicting Student Progression: The Influence of Race and Other Student and Institutional Characteristics on College Student Performance*. (ERIC Document Reproduction Service No. ED 220 058).

Green, R. L. (1991). *African-American Males: Education or Incarceration*. Battle Creek, MI: Kellogg Foundation. (ERIC Document Reproduction Service No. ED 346 184).

Guba, E. (1978). *Toward a Method of Naturalistic Inquiry in Educational Evaluation*. Los Angeles: Center for the Study of Evaluation.

Hacker, A. (1992). *Two Nations: Black, White, Separate, Hostile, Unequal*. New York: Scribner's.

"Introducing Thomas A. Fleming: National Teacher of the Year." (1992, December). *Ebony*, 68–70.

Johnson, J. H., and Bennett, L., Jr. (1992). *Succeeding Against the Odds: The Autobiography of a Great American Businessman*. New York: Amistad.

King, J. E., and Mitchell, C. A. (1990). *Black Mothers to Sons: Juxtaposing African-American Literature with Social Practice*. New York: Peter Lang.

Kunjufi, J. (1986). *Motivating and Preparing Black Youth for Success*. Chicago: African American Images.

Kunjufi, J. (1989). *Critical Issues in Educating African-American Youth*. Chicago: African American Images.

Lakoff, G., and Johnson, M. (1980). *Metaphors We Live By*. Chicago: University of Chicago Press.

Lakoff, G., and Turner, M. (1989). *More Than Cool Reason*. Chicago: University of Chicago Press.

Lincoln, Y., and Guba, E. (1985). *Naturalistic Inquiry*. Newbury Park, CA: Sage.

Littlejohn-Blake, S. M., and Darling, C. A. (1993). "Understanding the Strengths of African American Families." *Journal of Black Studies*, 23 (4), 460–471.

Mahoney, M. E. (1993). *Mentors: The President's Report*. New York: Commonwealth Fund.

Majors, R., and Billson, J. M. (1992). *Cool Pose: The Dilemmas of Black Manhood in America*. New York: Lexington.

Manns, W. (1988). "Supportive Role of Significant Others in Black Families." In H. P. McAdoo (Ed.), *Black Families*. Newbury Park, CA: Sage.

McAdoo, H. P. (ed.). (1988). *Black Families*. Newbury Park, CA: Sage.

McAdoo, J. L., and McAdoo, J. B. (1994). "The African-American Father's Role Within the Family." In R. G. Major and J. U. Gordon (Eds.), *The American Black Male: His Present Status and His Future*. Chicago: Nelson-Hall.

McCall, N. (1994). *Makes Me Wanna Holler: A Young Black Man in America*. New York: Random House.

McEwen, M. K., Roper, L. D., Bryant, D. R., and Langa, M. J. (1990). "Incorporating the Development of African-American Students into Psychosocial Theories of Student Development." *Journal of College Student Development*, 31, 429–435.

Myrdal, G. (1962). *An American Dilemma*. New York: Harper & Row.

Nettles, M. T. (1997). *The African American Education Data Book*. Fairfax, VA: Frederick D. Patterson Research Institute College Fund/UNCF.

Nettles, M. T., with Thoeny, A. R. (1988). *Toward Black Undergraduate Student Equality in American Higher Education*. Westport, CT: Greenwood Press, 1988.

Nettles, M. T., Thoeny, A. R., and Gosman, E. J. (1986). "Comparative and Predictive Analysis of Black and White College Achievement and Experiences." *Journal of Higher Education*, 57 (3), 289–318.

Patton, M. Q. (1987). *How to Use Qualitative Methods in Evaluation*. Newbury Park, CA: Sage.

Pollard, D. S. (1989). "Against the Odds: A Profile of Academic Achievers from the Urban Underclass." *The Journal of Negro Education*, 58 (3), 297–308.

Prothrow-Stith, D. (1993). *Deadly Consequences: How Violence Is Destroying Our Teenage Population and a Plan to Begin Solving the Problem*. New York: Harper Perennial.

Roebuck, J. B., and Murty, K. (1993). *Historically Black Colleges and Universities: Their Place in Higher Education*. Westport, CT: Praeger.

Schoem, D. (1991, April 3). "College Students Need Thoughtful, In-Depth Study of Race Relations." *The Chronicle of Higher Education*, p. A48.

Schulz, D. A. (1991). *Coming Up as a Boy in the Ghetto*. In D. Y. Wilkinson and R. L. Taylor (Eds.), *The Black Male in America: Perspectives on His Status in Contemporary Society*. Chicago: Nelson-Hall.

Slater, R. B. (1994). "The Growing Gender Gap in Black Higher Education." *The Journal of Blacks in Higher Education*, 3, 52–59.

Spencer, M., Brookins, G., and Allen, W. R. (eds.). (1985). *Beginnings: The Social and Affective Development of Black Children*. Hillsdale, NJ: Lawrence Erlbaum.

Staples, R. (ed.). (1991). *The Black Family: Essays and Studies*. Belmont, CA: Wadsworth.

Steel, R. (1991). *Mentoring: An Effective Tool for Retention of Minorities*. (ERIC Document Reproduction Service No. Ed 342 841).

Steward, R. J., Jackson, M. R., Sr., and Jackson, J. D. (1990). "Alienation and Interactional Styles in a Predominantly White Environment: A Study of Successful Black Students." *Journal of College Student Development*, 31, 509–515.

Taylor, R. L. (1989). "Black Youth, Role Models and the Social Construction of Identity." In R. L. Jones (Ed.), *Black Adolescents*. Berkeley: Cobb & Henry.

Thomas, G. E. (ed.) (1981). *Black Students in Higher Education, Conditions and Experiences in the 1970s*. Westport, CT: Greenwood Press.

United Negro College Fund. (1988–1989, Winter). "College Crisis of Black Males." *Research Trends*, 2 (1), 1.

"University Helping Blacks to Graduate." (1996, December 1). *The New York Times*, A 43.

Weber, J. (1992). "Creating the Environment for Minority Student Success: An Interview with Jacqueline Fleming." *Journal of Developmental Education*, 16 (2), 20–24.

West, C. (1994). *Race Matters*. New York: Vintage.

Willie, C. V., and Edmonds, R. R. (eds.) (1978). *Black Colleges in America: Challenge, Development, Survival*. New York: Teachers College Press.

Wilson-Sadberry, K. R., Winfield, L. F., and Royster, D. A. (1991). "Resilience and Persistence of African-American Males in Postsecondary Enrollment." *Education and Society*, 24 (1), 87–102.

Wright, R. (1945). *Black Boy*. New York: Harper.

Index

Achievement motivation theories in cross-cultural research, 50–55
Addison, Richard B., 19
African-American males: in crisis, 6, 25; in HBCUs and PWI, 9–11; in prison, 6; in single-parent homes, 7, 45–46, 56
African-American males in the study (Cluster I), 3, 29, 46, 55–60, 65–67, 70–71
African-American women enrolled in college, 13–14
Alexander v. Holmes County Board of Education, 17–18
Allen, W. R., 9–10, 47
Allwood, Shelton H., 9
American Missionary Association (AMA), 16, 17
Analytic memos, 23, 34–35
Antebellum period, 15–16
Armstrong, General S. C., 16
Ascher, C., 7
Ashley, Vincent, 31

Bennett, Lerone, Jr., 41
Bethlehem Baptist Association, 26
Billingsley, A., 42
Billson, J. M., 1, 2, 6
Biographical profile form, 28, 30

Black church, 17, 18, 27, 41–43, 68
Black colleges versus white colleges for the black student, 9–11
Black higher education, historical perspective, 15–18
Bonding, 26, 41, 45, 46, 65, 66, 67. *See also* Emergent findings
Booker, S., 5–6
Bowdoin College, 17
Bowser, B. P., 43–45
Brookins, G., 47
Brown v. Board of Education, 17
Bryant, D. R., 10
Bucknell University, 12

Caring, 26, 65, 66, 67, 69, 72
Carnoy, M., 12
Castenell, L., 50–53
Categories of the study, 34
Cheatham, H. E., 42–43, 45
Children of the Dream, 6
Choices, 26, 64, 65, 66, 67
Civil Rights Act of 1964, 17
Clark, Kenneth, 7
Clark, R., 43
Clency, Charles, C., 31
Cleveland State University, 8; minority mentoring program, 8

About the Author

MARILYN J. ROSS is Professor of Higher Education at Florida Memorial College in Miami.

ISBN 0-89789-535-5

HARDCOVER BAR CODE